TRADING R

TRADING RULES

THE ROAD TO MARKET WISDOM

William F. Eng

PITMAN PUBLISHING
128 Long Acre, London WC2E 9AN

A Division of Pearson Professional Limited

Trading Rules by William F. Eng, © 1990 by
Dearborn Financial Publishing, Inc.
Trading Rules II by William F. Eng, © 1995 by
Dearborn Financial Publishing, Inc.

First published in Great Britain 1995

© Pearson Professional Ltd, 1995

Authorized edition for sale in Europe
and Middle East only.

British Library Cataloguing in Publication Data
A CIP catalogue record for this book can be obtained
from the British Library.

ISBN 0 273 62218 8

1 3 5 7 9 10 8 6 4 2

Typeset by Pantek Arts, Maidstone, Kent.
Printed and bound in Great Britain by
Redwood Books Limited, Trowbridge, Wiltshire

*The Publishers' policy is to use paper manufactured
from sustainable forests.*

I wish to dedicate this book to two people.
My son, Alden, who just turned one year of age.
And to a special trader who passed away years ago.
As there is life, there is a death.
When one cycle ends, another begins.

CONTENTS

LIST OF FIGURES

INTRODUCTION

One morning in the summer of 1982 I was eating breakfast in the Chicago Board of Trade's lower level dining room when I saw David Goldberg, a partner at Goldberg Brothers. David and his brother, Robert, who later became chairman of the Chicago Board of Trade, presciently saw the growth of options trading. They emphasized clearing operations in the developing markets. Equity options began trading in 1973 at the Chicago Board Options Exchange. Since that time, the Goldberg clearing operation had been one of the top five clearing firms.

David was sitting alone, so I walked over with my tray of food and asked if I could join him for breakfast. He looked startled, for he had been deep in thought, but he invited me to sit down. We discussed briefly how things were going, and then he changed the subject and began talking about how long it took to be a successful trader a the Chicago Board of Trade.

"It's so tough for a trader to get into the business now. A young guy has to come in with $100,000 to cover his first three years of trading." Then he glanced at his watch, guzzled the last drops of his black coffee, and said, "I have to go, Bill. Bonds opened half an hour ago. I've go to talk to Bill Cousins." He pushed his chair back and walked briskly out of the cafeteria.

I sat there looking at the space that David had just occupied. I had managed to take some time from his life and got valuable nuggets of information. Cousins was the margin clerk for Goldberg clearing operations. He was responsible for watching the traders' positions and for checking the daily runs. When he had to, he physically yanked traders out of the pit and liquidated their positions. At times like these, traders lost control of their accounts. They froze in the pits as their equity eroded rapidly. One day they have several thousand dollars in their accounts and the next day they owe the clearing firm money.

For the rest of the day I watched the bonds move up. They finally bottomed after moving away from the secondary bottom created several weeks earlier. This upside move was in earnest. The five-year bear market had ended. Over the years I had trained myself to follow major trends. I realized that the bonds made a secondary bottom and removed myself from the bond pit. When markets end a long trending, one-directional move, I always found myself continuing to trade in the direction of the previous trend. In my own trading I always lost money when the markets bottomed or topped out.

I was not the only one to trade like this. I wondered who in the pit was still trading against this bond upmove. A week earlier Ricky "the Rocket" Barnes had bought the bottom. The traders he bought from either covered their shorts by buying them in at higher prices, or elsewere completely out of the game. I had sold some at the bottom, but I covered them when the market went up afterwards. Another trader was not so fortunate. He sold 200 bonds at the bottom and then got nailed by the ensuing violent upswing.

Two days after my breakfast talk with David Goldberg, I was sitting in the traders' lounge at the Trans Union building. The markets were quiet, and we all sat there checking the Quotron machines for price movements. Suddenly a trader from the options floor came up to me and asked if I had heard what happened to Larry Thomas. I shrugged my shoulders and said, "No, I haven't talked to him for about a week. I've got to call him though. We're trying to get a deck together to handle the new bean options that are going to trade soon. We plan to make some solid money." The trader looked at me and asked, "Didn't you hear? He committed suicide. He shot himself in the head Sunday."

Stunned, I looked at the trader. I looked but did not see. I breathed but did not exhale. The trader explained that Larry Thomas had sold bonds short Friday morning; then the bonds went up and he sold more. He lost between $50,000 and $70,000 before the day was over. Despondent over his trading losses, he drank heavily that weekend. He called his parents and argued with them. He discovered that he did not love his girlfriend. His childhood frustrations cropped up. With the mounting pressure to succeed in trading, in relationships, in life, he broke. He put the muzzle of his gun to his mouth and pulled the trigger Sunday night.

Even as I write this book six years later, I still feel the loss of a close friend.

The week before his death, Larry and I had talked about the bonds. I told him to be careful about trading on the bear side. He called me "Professor." Over the years I taught him how to count the waves in the Elliott wave theory. I taught him Gann analysis. He was

> *Hope coupled with knowledge of trading techniques and discipline will make you a winner in the markets.*

an eager student and he learned well. I taught him technical analysis, yet my message failed to enter his mind.

Death is a fact of life. Over the years I have befriended traders who committed suicide over losses caused by market action. I can remember the names and faces of four traders who ended their lives in such desolation. Larry Thomas was someone special to me. I saw in him my own life at the start of my trading career. He struggled to make money, just as I did when I started. I saw him search for knowledge, as I did when I failed in trading. I saw the successful trading techniques come to fruition for him, as they did for me when I traded the markets correctly.

What Larry Thomas did was exceptional. He lacked that one quality that all successful traders must have. He lacked hope.

With hope you can overcome obstacles. With hope you can do all the things you thought you could not do. With hope, the worst losers can ride the biggest bull markets. With hope, Larry could have succeeded in whatever he considered important in his life. With hope, he could even have come back from failure.

Hope alone, however, does not guarantee success. Hope coupled with knowledge of trading techniques and discipline will make you a winner in the markets.

I've compiled a list of 57 trading rules and thoughts that I consider the best I have seen over the years. I have illustrated each trading rule with examples that will help you recognize situations where you can use the rules. However, you must use caution when applying these rules. Indiscriminate application of rules, regardless of market stages, is very dangerous. It is akin to driving a car in a three-dimensional world with one eye shut. You'll be all over the place, with no clear sense of where you want to go.

With the information from this book you will be on the road to market knowledge. With that knowledge you can trade successfully for the rest of your lives. Without it, you might as well go into another business.

Good luck in your trading. Remember, it's only a game.

ACKNOWLEDGMENTS

I wish to thank Tim Slater, of Computrac, for the use of the output of Version 2.8 to illustrate parts of this book. Similar thanks go to William Forsyth and Steven Achelis, of Equis International, for use of the MetaStock Professional output to illustrate other parts. Thanks go to Jack Hutson, publisher of *Stocks and Commodities* magazine, for the use of the liquidity data chart.

Thanks to all my students who have expressed interest in becoming more proficient traders. Their questions and weaknesses showed me what my weaknesses as an educator were. I hope the knowledge that they gain from my writings and trading philosophies enriches their lives. The fact that they can make money in the markets will make them more helpful to others who are less talented. Not everyone wants to be a trader; yet everyone needs help—sometime, somewhere.

And final thanks to all the market analysts who have gone before me. Without their knowledge and techniques, the writing of this book would have been difficult, if not impossible.

Views expressed in this publication are solely those of the author and are not to be construed as the views of the Chicago Board of Trade, nor is the Chicago Board of Trade in any way responsible for the contents thereof.

"Would you tell me, please, which way I ought to go from here?" said Alice to the rabbit.

"That depends a good deal on where you want to get to," replied the rabbit to Alice.

Lewis Carroll, *Alice in Wonderland*

RULE 1

DIVIDE YOUR TRADING CAPITAL INTO TEN EQUAL RISK SEGMENTS

This rule of money management is widely credited to William D. Gann, the author and trader who developed innovative trading methods in the early part of this century. I have monitored my own trading results and modified this approach to equity management even further. If you follow my approach, you will never run out of trading capital, no matter how badly you trade.

Let's think about this rule and the situation surrounding it. You open a trading account with a finite amount of capital. With this capital you wish to take risks and make more money. In essence, what you are doing is putting your money into the market, a pool of funds, and acquiring an interest in it. If someone is willing to pay you more for your interest in the markets, then you sell your interests for a profit. It's as simple as that.

When you start to trade the markets, you should enter trades as if you expect to win on every one. It's important to have confidence in the success of your trades. If you don't, you will never trade risky positions, and those are the ones that have the greatest potential for profits. Nonetheless, you can't realistically expect that each trade will turn into a winner. The markets have many ways to make you lose money.

The only real winner in the market in the long term is the market itself. But individual traders are finite and must view the markets in shorter terms. It is in the shorter term that individual traders can profit. The problem with random walk theorists is they have no clear definition of time perspectives. They claim that there is no need to analyze the markets because all market movements are random. The purchase of any stock will give an advantage return over the life of the holdings.

The saying, "Take time out from trading. You can always go back to it," implies that the markets will always be there. An undisciplined trader who trades even in bad times offers the market the opportunity to outlive his other trading equity.

As an individual trader you are finite and you have finite trading equity. The market, on the other hand, is a conglomeration of many traders and has infinite resources. It can match you dollar for dollar. If you lost a dollar and the market lost a dollar, it would still have the superior position.

If you think of the trading game as one in which you are trading against the market, you will see what I mean. If you make a dollar, somebody in the market lost a dollar. If the markets are now worth a trillion dollars, you cannot accumulate all the profits of the market valuation in your lifetime. Not so with what you can lose. You can lose a dollar and the market will suck it up and demand more. You can lose all your trading equity, and the market will meander about looking for more equity from traders like yourself. In short, you can probably win a finite amount of money from the market, but you can definitely lose all that you have. It makes sense to limit your exposure to market losses.

The problem rests with how much exposure of trading equity you should risk. How much money are you willing to let the market take away from you before you take your money and put it elsewhere? From my experience in the futures market, the maximum amount that I feel comfortable risking is no more than 2.5 percent of my total trading capital on any one position. Some of you may laugh at this extremely conservative number.

The maximum to risk on any one trade is the recommended 10 percent. Anything more than that will mathematically affect your ability to survive even a modest string of losses. If you risk a flat rate of 10 percent of your initial trading capital, you will have a 1/64 chance of losing all ten trades. One chance in 64 of ten straight losing trades is low. With this probability you should be able to get a winner somewhere in the string of ten trades. Then the question gets down to whether the amount won on the winners is enough to offset the losses on the losers.

> *The maximum risk on any one trade is the recommended 10 percent. If you risk a flat rate of 10 percent of your initial capital, you will have a 1/64 chance of losing all ten trades.*

I have modified the flat 10 percent of total starting capital to be a percentage of the remaining balance in your trading account. In this way, there will never be a zero balance in your account. To carry out this strategy, you need merely take a percentage of your remaining balance as the amount risked on each trade.

There are two distinctly different ways of measuring winners. I make a distinction between winning trades and dollar amount won on the winners. In the course of making a trade, if the position shows a tick profit, most people would consider this a winner. Technically, it is a winner, but you will need a series of these to be able to make a substantial profit. I would rather trade a minimum one lot and squeeze the trade for many ticks before I consider the trade a winner. This is being harder on myself because I must not only initiate a trade that shows a minimum one tick profit, but also generate many more tick profits before I can consider it a winner.

Another point enters into the rationing of risk positions and exposing your capital to risk. If you went to Las Vegas and played the roulette wheel, you would find that in the long run you would wind up losing money. That's because of the 36 numbers that you can bet on, 17 are black and 17 are red. There are two numbers that belong to the house. With two to the house, you have slightly less than an even chance of winning if you just bet on the colors. If the house removed the two extra numbers so that you had exactly a 50 percent chance of winning when betting on colors only, your longterm chances would have improved dramatically. Would you play the game under such conditions?

The foolhardy gambler would rationalize that he now has the same chances of winning that the house has: an even chance. The smart gambler, however, would recognize the very subtle difference derived from the odds, which are not shown in the mere probabilities of the roulette wheel. This subtle difference is based on the theory of runs. Let's assume that you had a capital base of $10,000 to play the roulette wheel. At perfectly even odds you would still be at a disadvantage based on the amount of capital that the house has at its disposal. If the house has a capital base of $10,000,000 to play against you; you would find that eventually you would lose your $10,000. If you experienced a run of bad trades, you could lose all your betting capital of $10,000, and you would be out of the game. If the house loses $10,000 first to you, your capital would have doubled from $10,000 to $20,000. The house still has $9,990,000 left. What I am talking about here is a streak of losses. With $10,000,000 of capital at the house's disposal it can stand a series of 1,000 losses of $10,000. If you have one streak of a $10,000 loss, you are out of the game.

You must divide your risk capital into equal risk segments of 10 percent or less, preferably a defined percentage of declining equity balance. Then you must push the odds of successful trading to better than 50 percent in your favor. Just to obtain even odds will cause you to lose money in the end.

RULE 2

USE A TWO-STEP ORDER PROCESS

Thomas Temple Hoyne published a book in 1922 titled *Speculation: Its Sound Principles and Rules for Its Practice.* Imagine my surprise when he mentioned this trading strategy, which I developed for myself with my own resources. When he placed an order to enter a market, he also entered a stop loss order at the same time. He called this his two-order rule. The fact that someone else already thought of this trading strategy before me only serves to validate it. *Certain trading techniques and approaches span all markets through all time.* They have obvious applications in profitable trading strategies.

Losses will take you out of the market faster than a margin clerk. Profits won't. From this standpoint alone, it is critical that you provide some mechanism in your trading that will prevent your losses from becoming insurmountable. I use stop loss orders to prevent total erosion of my trading capital.

Stop loss orders are entered with your broker. The broker executes them when the market price moves to that level. The stop sell order is executed when the price reaches down and hits your stop price; the broker sells out your position. If the price reaches up to your stop buy price, the broker is obligated to buy in your position. You must make a distinction between a stop loss order and a stop loss *limit* order. In the case of a simple stop loss order, once the price on your limit is reached, the order is executed at the prevailing market price. With the stop loss limit order, once the price of your limit is reached, the order is executed at the price that is specified on the order. The problem with this type of

5

order is that the actual market may have moved away from the limit price so your order may not actually be executable. Different exchanges accept different types of stop orders. You must check with your exchange and your broker to see if they will accept the orders that you want to enter.

My personal feeling is to use stop orders that are triggered when the limit is reached and executed at the prevailing market price. The object of the stop order is to limit losses because of bad market judgment. If the price of the item you are trading is going against you, you have to get out at any cost. Don't play for price at this point; play for position: The original pricing of your position is obviously wrong, so get out of it. Get back in later at a better price.

Most traders use stop loss limit orders to close out opposite positions. If they are short, they enter a stop buy order to prevent the price from reaching higher and damaging their equity further. The converse is true with long positions. They use stop sell orders to prevent erosion of their capital.

Some experienced traders use stop limit orders to initiate positions instead of closing them out. These orders are often placed outside of trading ranges. When the orders are executed, the traders expect a continuation in the direction of the breakout of the trading range. For example, if a stock has been trading between $5 and $10 for several months, the experienced trader enters a stop limit by order at $10.25. This order is executed when the stock trades above the $10 level and touches $10.25. The trader speculates on the strength of the stock. If the price of the stock has enough power to break through the trading range to the upside, it is showing enough strength to continue beyond $10.25.

The conventional wisdom concerning stop loss orders centers around using price as the triggering number. This is not always the case. Some traders use time as the trigger for liquidating positions. The Market Profile® technique developed and made popular by Peter Steidlmayer uses the passage of time as the limiting factor. If one were to trade using the Market Profile®

Market Profile® is a registered trademark of the Chicago Board of Trade, which holds exclusive rights to the Market Profile® graphics.

technique, one would expect some major occurrence to happen with the confines of the trading day. If this expected occurrence does not happen within a certain time frame, the position is closed out no matter where the price is at.

Financial astrologers, the esoteric market traders, use time as an entry and exit factor. At certain times of the day or week they will enter positions because their trading techniques call for market entry.

So we have seen the application of stop loss orders as defined by either price or time. There are also rare cases

> *The real problem is where to place stops. Remember that the two-order rule is not invalidated by market movements that take you out of a winning position.*

where stop loss orders can be defined by trading volume. In fact, the only viable technique for tracking market activity through volume is the one developed by Joseph Granville—On-Balance Volume (OBV). On-Balance Volume, in a simple sense, is a cumulation of up volume versus down volume on a particular stock or futures contract. Over time, the cumulation forms a trending zigzag-shaped chart. When the OBV shows accumulation, independent of what the price at that particular coinciding time is, OBV practitioners can use the upside volume breakouts as buy indicators and enter the market using this as the signal. There is a problem with using OBV breakout points as a type of stop loss order because they do not offer enough time to liquidate positions. Hence, the OBV technique is effective only on the buy side.

We have discussed the use of stops as a critical factor in market success. Some investors might counter and say that they have placed stops, which were then executed, only to see the market resume in the other direction. This, unfortunately, reinforces their original decision to center the market on the right side. After the slight retracement, which was enough to catch their stop, they have no position in a correctly analyzed market. If you think about why you use stops—to limit losses on backtrades—you will realize that your stop was triggered because price went against your position, not because your position was bad.

The real problem is where to place the stops. Remember that the viability of the two-order rule is not invalidated by market movements that take you out of a winning position. What this means is that you don't know where to place the stops correctly.

Let's look at one extreme case of stop placement. Several years ago, when I was a broker with a small brokerage firm, I had a client who was a hog producer. He needed to use the futures markets to hedge the price of his hogs. The markets were bullish, and as long as they went up he didn't really need to sell any of his hog production. We decided to place a trailing stop and follow the market up. This allowed the markets to stop him out into a long cash hogs/short futures hogs hedge when it topped out. Even here we weren't sure where to place the trail stop. Do we place it 10 percent below the previous market close, after a major key reversal day, or use one of the countless other approaches that were then available?

I settled on something very basic for sheer lack of any definitive number to use as a limit. Every day we ratcheted the stop loss order up to a fraction of a cent above a limit down move. Futures contracts in the United States have limit moves. In past hog markets, when the price reversed from a sustained one-directional move, it went limit. Therefore, if the hogs had enough weakness to sell off the first time, I wanted to have the hogs hedged right then and there. Well, the first time the market broke, it did go limit down, and we were hedged perfectly. In a purely mechanical way we hedged our cash production and used a minimum of market analysis.

The above anecdote illustrates one simple fact of using stop loss orders: Regardless of what you think about your market, you must have a stop loss order somewhere. It can be 10 percent of market price or whatever number you want. It might even be as ridiculous as half of current market price! I have seen enough market moves to know that even the ridiculous becomes patently sound given the right market conditions. Had you used a simple 25 percent of last previous price prior to the stock market meltdown of October 1987, you would have retained a good portion of your profits.

RULE 3

DON'T OVERTRADE

Overtrading was a problem that took me a long time to overcome because I didn't know what I was looking for. Let me recount a story about a trader at the Chicago Board of Trade that illustrates how serious a problem veteran traders regard overtrading to be.

A second generation floor trader had DOT as his badge acronym although those letters were not the initials of his name, William Jones. While trading in the Major Market Index (MAXI) pit one day, I heard the trader's father say "And remember, don't overtrade." That's what DOT meant: Don't overtrade! I thought it was a clever idea to incorporate a trading rule into an acronym. Little did I know that this brief trading rule would be critical to my own survival in the pits.

If you have been trading for a long time, you know that overtrading is a ubiquitous problem. And if you have ever tapped out of the trading profession, the chances are that you got yourself into trouble by overtrading. You lost more money than you had in your account.

When I was trading full time, I took naps in the clearing firm's lounge. One particularly grueling morning I dozed off in a couch next to Robert Goldberg's office. Robert was a partner in the Goldberg Brothers company. When I awoke I overheard him call a phone clerk on the bond floor and give an order to sell five contracts. I found it strange that a partner in a multimillion dollar clearing operation would be trading a mere five lot.

Four years later I was in the MAXI pit trading my usual twos and threes. Peter Steidlmayer, developer of the Market Profile® trading technique, walked into the pit and offered a one lot, then

9

another one. He sold a total of five contracts and walked away from the pit. Later in the day the market moved against his position, so he came back into the pit and bought five contracts back. I sold him a couple contracts and, as I was carding the trade, he told me that he had to close out all his trades. The total commitment to his analysis was five short contracts, and he bought them all in. I was puzzled at the small size these two extremely well-capitalized traders initiated, but I later found out that it's not the size of your trades, but how you trade your winners and losers. I have heard the statement, "Size kills," often in the pits. These two traders knew what this meant.

> *You can get into trouble by not knowing that you're overtrading. You can buy low-priced items for cash, but when items get higher-priced, the sellers make them more attractive to a cash-poor buying public by offering payment programs and credit terms.*

Let me explain what overtrading means and how you can get into trouble by not knowing that you're overtrading.

You can buy low-priced items for cash, but when the items get higher-priced, the sellers make them more attractive to a cash-poor buying public by offering payment programs and credit terms. This means that you can buy a high-priced item for a fraction of its total cost and then make payments on it until the balance is paid off. People buy food on a cash basis and they buy high-priced items like cars and real estate on a credit basis.

Since there is no basic need to buy stocks or futures as there is to buy clothing, food, or shelter, sellers of stocks or futures offer "credit" terms as an inducement to prospective buyers. You can buy any number of stocks or futures by merely putting a small percentage of the total purchase price in your trading account. In stocks, this small percentage is called margin money. In futures, it is called a "good faith" deposit. In both cases, the money you use to control 100 percent of the stocks or futures is a small percentage of the total purchase price. The balance is to be paid off on demand.

This evolved into leverage, whereby a small amount of capital can be used to control a larger piece of assets. For stocks, margin has run from a low of 5 percent to as high as 75 percent. So from a low of $5 to a high of $75, you could control $100 worth of stocks. When the $100 worth of stocks gains $10 in value to a total market value of $110, the full cash buyer would receive a 10 percent return. The margin buyer who makes an investment of $5 would make $10 in this particular situation, or a 200 percent return. If margin is 75 percent, then $75 is required to control $100 worth of stock. A $10 return on a $75 investment amounts to a 13.33 percent return. Hence, you can see how margin benefits the investor.

> *You can buy any number of stocks or futures by merely putting a small percentage of the total purchase price in your trading account. In stocks, this small percentage is called margin money. In futures, it is called a "good faith" deposit.*

In the futures markets, there are no margin requirements. Instead, the industry works with good faith deposits, which speculators must have at all times in their trading account. The deposits range from 3 percent to 10 percent of the actual market value of the futures contract. For all practical purposes, the deposits are similar in function to margin: They allow you to control more assets that you could buy outright.

Leverage also works against investors or speculators when the price of the investment or speculation goes against them. I've illustrated how an appreciating price multiplies the returns. If the price of the asset deteriorates, a cash buyer loses a percentage of the full $100. A loss of $5 means a 5 percent loss. A loss of $10 means a loss of 10 percent. The margin buyer encounters fast deterioration of capital when the price of the asset drops. The 10 percent margin buyer would only have to put up $10 to control $100 worth of stocks. If the stock drops from $100 to $95, which is a 5 percent loss of the original market value, the margin buyer at 10 percent would suffer a 50 percent loss of his or her $10 investment. A $10 loss would mean a full 100 percent loss of the investment. If the price drops $15, from $100 to $85, the cash buyer would sustain a 15 percent loss; the margin buyer at 10 percent would sustain the full loss of the $10 margin money, and an additional $5. Such is the way margin, or good faith deposit, works. This little exercise in the mechanics of margins and good faith deposits is not without reason. One of the dangers of trading has always been overtrading. The business of trading is to make the stocks or futures reasonably priced so more people can invest and speculate. You can expect that margin and good faith deposits are used extensively in the business.

Let's move on to futures contracts to continue the discussion. Good faith deposits are calculated with a basic formula: Bring in the greatest number of market participants without getting them too highly leveraged. The greater the number of traders and players in the futures market, the more money the exchanges make through sales of data, commissions, and transaction fees. Even though exchanges are set up as nonprofit organizations, they continue to survive and thrive. When prices are low, the margins are low. There is less daily volatility, so a minimum amount will cover the volatility. In such situations, there are fewer market players, so there is no need to worry about the players not having enough money to cover market losses.

When prices get high, the exchanges and cleaning firms increase the good faith deposits to weed out the undercapitalized traders. It also protects the trader's account from getting wiped out by daily price volatility.

RULE 4

NEVER OVERTRADE, EVEN IF YOU'RE A CORPORATE TREASURER

The use of derivatives has increased the problem of overtrading. As we trade globally and geographic borders between nations give way to electronic superhighways, the problems of overtrading will persist and magnify.

Trading the markets correctly has always been very important. In our age of globalized finances, it becomes critical. One company president can take down a company over time with bad management decisions; one company treasurer with trading responsibilities can take down a company with one bad telephone call. If we are not careful, a federal treasurer can cause a government to collapse.

Disarming Disinterest Pervasive in the Management Community

In 1989, as I embarked upon my career as a financial writer, I submitted an outline for an article on the problems companies face when dealing with traders in their corporate treasury departments to the premier business management magazine in the world, the *Harvard Business Review*. In my covering letter I suggested the possibility that one person in a corporation could take down the whole company, a company which was created by the

13

sweat and effort of thousands of employees over the span of several generations. This singular person was identified as a trader in the treasury department of these companies, who with one single phone call could literally wipe out the existence of the company! The magazine turned down my article. In brief, they indicated that their subscribing managers would not be interested.

However, the need for this kind of article has not gone away. With attitudes such as those proffered by such a mainstream magazine, it comes as no surprise that some corporate management has allowed individual traders in corporate treasury departments to run amuck. I'd like to warn the treasurers that we have yet to see the worst of the financial derivatives debacle. Brace yourselves for a global collapse simply as a result of human nature. I've seen traders destroy themselves because they didn't know how to trade. Now, we're seeing corporate treasurers turned traders take tremendous risks unknowingly because they don't know how to trade.

My background is self-taught as a trader for my own account. From first hand experience, as member of several exchanges, stocks, options and futures, I saw a lot of traders take it on the chin when their positions went awry after market conditions went abruptly against them. In 1973, we saw the development of the first centralized stock options exchange, the Chicago Board of Options Exchange. Since then we have seen explosive growth in options trading.

As a trader I learned the hard way to discipline myself mentally from taking extraordinarily large positions with my limited capital. I learned *never to overtrade*, regardless of what I was trading: stocks, futures, or options. If you overtrade and lose, this is for keeps.

Derivatives Debacle Trilogy: Part One

I retired from active floor trading for my own account in 1986 to set up my writing career. From the sidelines I watched the unfolding of Part I of the first derivatives debacle of the trilogy, which the floor traders at the Chicago Board of Options Exchange faced in 1987. During the crash of 1987 when the Dow Jones Industrial Average dropped over 500 points, instead of proving to be a benefit, derivatives became the bane of some options traders' existence!

Overnight, previous option positions, which had neither long nor short market biases, exploded to infinite "long-sided" positions in a collapsing market.

That's the beauty and danger of leverage. With a lot of positions, the levarage can magnify geometrically when the underlying moves only fractionally. In the case of the dropping market, the underlying moved a lot, and the derivatives positions moved enough to bulge eyeballs, throb hearts, and twist larger intestines. A few of my trader friends were carted off the exchange floor that day never to be heard from or seen again.

> *I'm sure anybody in his most insane moment would not risk $5,000,000 in derivatives positions when he had only $100,000 in his trading account, but this very same person could unknowingly be longer and longer in a rapidly declining market based on his assumption, albeit wrong, of position risks.*

Shortly after the meltdown week, I saw future problems that could develop with indiscriminate use of leveraged trading products. And these products were foisted on naive and inexperienced treasurers who became traders overnight. But the mantle of trader is not a title handed over to an employeee along with the raise. It must be treated with greater respect. "Trader" must be earned through trial and error but without too much risk.

Some of these individual traders have created their own little fiefdoms, protecting and sheltering their roles and their departments with arcane terminology (forwards, straddles, rollovers, etc.) and even more, obscure strategies (delta neutral spreads, backspreads, iron butterflies, jelly rolls, etc.). In the late 1980s and the early 1990s, corporate management did not pay heed to the "whole heap of trouble" some of these traders were getting the other "9,999" employees into.

15

Being long a million shares isn't bad when the stock goes up. Being long one share is horrible when the stock goes down. The principle in both cases is the same: when you're right, you are right; when you are wrong, being committed to only a miniscule position is still absolutely wrong! This is all part of trading correctly.

Similarly, when 9,999 employees work hard to build up a company, that's excellent management; when all 9,999 employees go on strike, that's terrible management. When one employee goes awry, even though the rest are doing their jobs perfectly well, management is still at fault.

Part Two of the Derivative Battle

Although the magazine rejected the article because they considered the scope of the topic too narrow for their audience, I'm sure this topic is now of interest to their readers since we have just witnessed part two of the derivatives debacle.

The former treasurer of Orange County in California did what no successful trader should ever do: He lost sight of what his role was.

A man with such a position of control over so many assets, which did not personally belong to him, took a shot and lost a lot! He lost between $1.7 to $2 billion dollars, in a few short months, of the assets over which he had fiduciary responsibilities.

Recently, a single trader at Baring Securities of London managed to lose over $1.4 billion of the investment bank's money in less than two months' time, thus putting four thousand employees' jobs at risk. Ironically this trader did use good equity management. His $1.4 billion loss was derived from positions worth about $28 billion. That's only a mere 5 percent that the trader lost of the total positions. The 5 percent is within acceptable exposure parameters. Kudos to his skill at managing his equity exposure. Unfortunately, he used the leverage available with the futures contracts he traded. Using a presumed, and conservative, leverage of 10 percent cash controlling the other 90 percent of the futures contracts value, he multiplied his trading capital tenfold to 50 times! With multipliers as large as this one, it doesn't take much movement to get this trader and his position into deep trouble.

These two examples involved considerably more position risk, not necessarily more money, than a simple trader's account at the options exchange. I'm sure anybody in his most insane moment would not risk $5,000,000 in derivatives positions when he had only $100,000 in his trading account, but this very same person could unknowingly be longer and longer in a rapidly declining market based on his assumption, albeit wrong, of position risks. This is exactly how each of these traders exposed their assets: they were oblivious to position risk. In a sense, they overtraded without knowing it.

The second part of this trilogy involved off-exchange traded products which banks and brokerage companies created and sold, well away from the jurisdiction of the options exchanges' SEC-controlled environment! But these very same people in these banks and brokerage companies say that they don't want SEC or other government controls.

We all believe in the invisible hand guiding the markets. In the context of global markets and Darwinian survival, one could argue that Orange County deserved to perish. Orange County and her managers couldn't take the pressures so why should they exist? Who are these bankers and brokers kidding when they advocate this position? Give these clients the toy gun and expect them to stop at using caps? Most will, but a few others will move on to play with dangerous armaments. I don't worry about guys who stop at cap guns; I worry about those who drag us into global financial wars. And we are quickly approaching financial global warring.

The bankers and brokers are not going to take the responsibility of educating these clients on position risks. Witness how Merrill Lynch claimed their agency role in Citron's Orange County fiasco. However weak their argument, bankers' and brokers' defenses have always been based on their role of "agency." As agents of the corporations they aren't culpable for the products and services they have sold.

17

The second part of this trilogy has shown us only the tip of the iceberg. Someone must protect these traders and corporations from themselves, and secondly, prevent them from inflicting financial risk and harm to trusting beneficiaries. The solution: bring in government controls, reporting functions, and risk controls. I may be accused of limiting the free market arm in trading, but I won't be faulted for allowing individual traders who have no idea of the difficulty of trading correctly to take down whole companies. The game is no longer a simple buy or sell decision. The amount of financial power in the hands of the few have increased tremendously over the last few years of financial warring.

Part Three—What's next?

Implied in this call for stricter government control of the financial arena is the assumption some of these singular traders don't always know what they're doing. You're absolutely right in concluding that. Everybody can make money when the economy is booming. We don't hire these managers to do that in boom times: We hire them to cover our liability risks. If they want to speculate, they speculate on their own time and with their own money. They mustn't and cannot speculate with other people's money for which these treasurers have fiduciary responsibilities.

We now have two data points to help us plot the direction of international financial stress. The first was the 1987 stock options debacle at the beginning, with options traded on the Chicago Board Options Exchange. The second data point is the ongoing debacle in the derivatives markets. Municipalities with billions under control of their treasurers are suffering greatly because of their treasurers' inability to trade the markets safely. I'm not talking about trading markets well, for that requires years of trading experience. I'm merely talking about trading safely with a very keen eye toward position risks.

There are no controls imposed by these singular traders on themselves to limit position risks.

With two datapoints already in place we can draw a line. The trend line slopes toward larger and more stressful financial disasters in the trading areas. The individual exchange members got whacked. The corporate treasurers are getting their fill right now.

Where is the third data point to be found; where will the next derivatives debacle occur? This point has to be larger than exchange traders and corporate treasurers combined!

What are the largest entities? They are governments: large-scale, man-made institutions controlling the assets of millions of their constituents. Some in these governments do not know what position risks are. As an experienced trader, I know exactly my position risks when I initiate positions. Unfortunately, this experience came painfully slowly. Government employees can take down a government operation if they have not learned the patience of trading well.

Brace yourselves. This last derivative debacle will be one big one. In the interim, hone your trading skills. It will be the one time in history where government disgorges revenues to their constituents.

RULE 5

NEVER LET A PROFIT TURN INTO A LOSS

This is a simple enough rule that everybody applies thinking about. When a floor trader first told me about it I dismissed him as being overly cautious. I continued to make the mistake of selling out my winners and keeping my losers. As a young trader, my mistakes could be overcome; as I get older, the mistakes are more difficult to overcome.

Let's go through the process of placing a trade to illustrate how I manage to maintain a profit in it. When I make a decision to buy or sell a futures or a stock, I also figure out how much I am willing to risk on the trade.

Let's say I want to buy 100 shares of IBM at $124 per share. I figure out that I will put in a stop order at around the $121 level. The actual number is something like $120-7/8. Whole numbers and even fractions are where the public enters the markets; I stay away from public orders. There might be a lot of public orders resting at $121 to buy the stock, but all the orders to buy at that price won't be filled. If they are all filled at $121, there's a reason why informed insiders would be willing to sell all the public wants to buy at the $121 level. My selling out my position at $120-7/8 would be warranted because the price of the stock should drop pretty drastically after all the public orders to buy at the 121 support level are taken out.

Let's go back to the original scenario, where I buy stock at $124. I now enter an order to stop out my position at $120-7/8. At $120-7/8 I am taking a $3-1/8 risk. If the price does not drop to my stop price, then I must wait patiently for it to go up. The rule that cautions me not to let a profit turn into a loss tells me that once the price of the stock goes above my purchase price I must get rid of it if and when it starts to show a possibility of a loss. (*The rule does not tell me to get out of a winning position if it shows a profit!*) If the price reaches a high of $124-1/8, I must be willing to let it go at $124 if it ever dips back there. At $124-1/4 I must sell it if it gets back to $124. If it shoots up immediately to $130, I must sell it if it gets back to $124!

However, strict adherence to the rule is impractical for two reasons. The first reason is that markets never go straight up or down. If you bought a stock at $124, you can't realistically expect it to go straight up without any backing action. The second reason is that the cost of commissions to the outsider is too high relative to the minimum fluctuations. If commission costs are $50 for a one-sided execution on a 100-share trade at $124, the stock price would have to go up to $125 before you would break even. If you got out of the trade at the same price you went in, you would wind up a loser.

In this example I used a trailing $3-1/8 point stop, or whatever dollar amount I was willing to risk on that type of trade. That is, if the stock trades up to a high price of $125, I would move my stop up to $121-7/8, risking $3-1/8. If the stock trades up to $126, I would move my stop up to $122-7/8, still risking 3-1/8.

The subjective judgment comes in once the stock trades at or above $125. Here I would risk a potential loss of $2-1/8 from my original entry position of $124; at $126 I would risk a potential loss of $1-1/8 from my original entry position of $124. I am making a distinction between potential losses from entry price and the potential loss from the high move. The first case is oriented towards trading equity, independent of market action. In the second case, the profit valuation is based on trading equity plus a portion of the paper profits dependent on the high of the market's up move. My main objective is to preserve my initial equity. If I can maintain control of my equity, I will have greater control over market risks to my paper profits.

In either case—a $125 high or a $126 high—I would risk losing part of my equity. According to Rule 5, any deterioration of trading equity is not acceptable, so with the entry price at $124, my exit point must be at $124 if the trade goes against me.

The problem concerns the definition of a loss. At what price level or time span, relative to the entry level of my trade, do I have a loss?

> *I have always chosen the halfway mark as a balance. At a one-half retracement back, you have an even chance of being wrong or right. A one-third retracement back would be giving the market too little leeway in reactions.*

When you put on a trade, the potential loss must be taken out of your trading capital. If you buy stock at $124, you place a stop at a lower price. The difference between the entry price and the stop loss price is your potential loss.

When the trade you have put on starts to show a profit, at what point do you consider the paper profits apart of your trading capital that you can use to gauge potential losses? If the stock you bought at $124 is now at $130 and you still have the open position, you now have a paper profit of $6; on 100 shares of stock you show a profit of $600. At what point do you consider this $600, unrealized as it is, to be part of your trading capital?

This is hard to determine, and since you are dealing with capital, it isn't a question of mere semantics. If you consider your trading capital to be original capital less the paper profit, then you can let the price of the stock dip all the way back to $124 before you start to worry about a deteriation of your trading capital. If, on the other hand, you consider the $600 paper profit to be part of your trading equity, then once the price dips below $130, you will have sustained a loss. I settle on something in the middle when the price appreciates to a level where my position cannot be taken out at a loss if the trailing stop order is executed—I take half of the paper profits, as marked by the extreme of the move and use that as a stop point, give or take a few fractions. That is, with the initial entry price of $124 and a high swing of $130, I would place my stop at around the halfway mark—somewhere slightly below $127: $126-7/8 or $126-3/8. This is a rule of thumb to preserve some sort of profits. The actual stop price might be closer to the lower range of some important chart support point.

I have always chosen the halfway mark as a balance. At a one-half retracement back, you have an even chance of being wrong or right. A one-third retracement back would be giving the market too little leeway in reactions.The market often retraces one-third, only to resume its original direction. If you unload your position at a one-third retracement, you would be selling prematurely out of a bullish move. On the other hand, a two-thirds retracement would be offering the market too much of your profits. I have often found that if the market backs two-thirds, it is too weak to rally much. If this situation occurs, then it is a good idea to close out your positions.

Whatever frame of reference you use to determine whether market retracements have affected your profits, you must do it systematically. You can't consider a dip below the high of the swing to be a loss of profits on one trade and a dip to the halfway mark of your paper profits to be an erosion of profits on the next trade.

A systematic approach to valuing market losses is crucial in evaluating future market trends. The permutations of the markets are infinite and random, where as the methods of analyzing the markets are finite and must be systematic. Your goal as a successful trader must be to make the market less random and less infinite.

RULE 6

USE STOP LOSS ORDERS

According to a trading psychology book from the early 1900s, "Stop loss orders are most effective in the late stage of a Bull market. That is just the time to use extreme caution. In the early stages, however, 'stop losses' may sever you from the limb of the tree which you may be sitting on. The object of stops is to prevent losses and long tie-ups of capital."

The issue of whether or not to use stop loss orders has always been hotly debated. In my own case I've always used stop loss orders "to prevent losses and long tie-ups of capital." At times I might have been lax by not entering a stop loss order to protect my open position, but most of the time within three days of the execution of the entry order I've always had stop loss orders in place.

However, according to the above rule, note the market condition under which stop loss orders should not be used. The rules advise not to use stop loss orders in the early stages of a bull market because they assume that your position will be stopped out with losses while the market is building for a runaway stage later.

Yes, and no, is all I can say to this contention. I've always used stop loss orders in trading ranges which eventually turned out to be bases upon which massive bull markets spring forth. I've also used them in trending markets. I do not discriminate among the types of markets I trade: the stop loss orders are there always!

The positioning of my stop orders in trading range, base-building markets has always been far enough away from the general range of the market that these stop loss orders seldom got caught. If and when they do get caught, I always re-enter the market, so this precludes losing out on a bullish position in a base-building market. I take my wounds, but I also get back in.

This is a perfect example of employing a **set of strategies** that are so in tune with the markets that each strategy by itself points to an overall correct trading strategy: I enter long positions in base-building markets; I enter stop loss orders in case I am wrong; and if I am taken out of my positions, *I re-enter from the long side again.* The first rule by itself implies that the practitioner of the rule doesn't have a general trading strategy; that is, in base-building markets, entering a stop loss order will remove you from a long position before the market charges up. This rule implies that you will not re-enter the market long.

The sensitivity to some traders have to the type of markets they're trading, and whether or not they will have an increased or decreased chance of getting their stops caught, explains why these people have told me that they never place stop loss orders in the markets to protect their positions and wind up making huge profits!

Because these traders have always positioned in trading range markets, and not runaway markets, this allowed them the luxury of not using stop loss orders and still never setting themselves up for potentially huge losses. The damage done to one's open positions in trading range markets is minimal, with or without stop loss orders in place; in runaway markets, if and when the markets reverse, backing off can damage one's equity.

The two groups of traders—one using stops all the time and the other never using stops—are all basically entering positions at the base-building periods. Stops placed here, if entered at all, and then if caught, will close out their positions at minimal losses, but losses still. *In cases like these, taking the open positions without being stopped out is just as good, if not better than getting caught on the low of the trading range base with stop orders!* Especially if once you get caught on the stop you are inclined to go in the opposite direction, i.e., not continue to be long but to take the short position!

Without knowing it, these investors or traders have predefined their supposed "violation" of the stop loss rule. The conditions under which they don't use stop loss orders have minimized the chances of getting stopped out, and also have created a condition whereby they can get stopped out often on the low of the trading range lows and still climb back on board for a possible sustained move. So they are perfectly right in what they are propounding: no stop loss orders, ever, and it just so happens that these traders always position themselves in base-building markets.

> **Until your skills in assessing market conditions improve, you must use stops.**

This is part of the work that you as a thinking trader must do. Now that you've figured out that it is okay to never use stops because you only want to position in base-building markets, what are base-building markets? How do you know that the long position, not protected by a stop loss order, will not collapse if the market breaks away to the downside? If you are trading stocks, there is some sort of intrinsic value the market doesn't trade under. For example, how much lower can a $2 stock go?

Unfortunately, value in the futures market is not based on something as abstract as earnings and sales, but rather on utility value. In the two commodities of corn and wheat, wheat prices historically trade above the price of corn. If the supply of wheat is great, the price will go down below the price of corn until the wheat can be used as feed for livestock, at which price it should stop going down. That's the utility value. If corn prices, however, go lower than the wheat, so will wheat prices. What does a trader do in cases like these where there is a limitless bottom to the price of wheat? This has occurred infrequently, probably no more than four or five times in the history of recorded prices from the Chicago Board of Trade.

Now you can understand the problem with trying to being so precise about applying rules to the markets based on other pre-existing conditions. It makes more sense, and is more practical, to just slap on the positions and place the stop loss order far enough that it won't get caught in a normal reaction. Why bother to think about the market condition of your order? It is important to know whether or not you're in a breakout stage or in a runaway market, but by indiscriminately placing stop loss orders you will absolutely protect your equity whether your analysis is correct or not and ultimately, whether or not you have gauged the current market condition to be either trending or trading. Until your skills in assessing market conditions improve, you must use stops. Even after you've developed such assessment skills, you should still use stops!

"Use stops indiscriminately" might be the wrong phrase to use here, but it highlights my point that you must use safe-guards, regardless of how inane, in the markets.

To trade otherwise is to add to the complexity of the analysis, something to which a trader like myself is averse.

RULE 7

TRADE WITH THE TREND

An experience I had driving the notorious "S" curve on Chicago's Lake Shore Drive about ten years ago showed me that moving with the trend can be a basic survival strategy on many different levels.

Before it was redesigned, this curve was the scene of many accidents because of the two sharp turns that gave it more of a "Z" shape. Returning home after a rough day of trading, I was a bit sloppy in steering the car around the narrow-laned curve. First I crossed the white dividing line on the left; then I overshot the right dividing line in my lane and had to veer again sharply back to the left.

As I shifted the car back and forth, trying to avoid an accident on either side, I had a visual image of what "trading with the trend" was all about. Over the years, this rule helped me make a lot of money in the markets. As long as I stayed within my own lane and progressed with the traffic, I eventually got to the end. When other drivers veered sharply out of their lanes, they crashed into other cars. The markets are similar to this. Once a market is in a defined trend, you must trade with the directions of that market. If you fail to do this, you will have many accidents.

The markets are in one of two stages at any given point in time: They are either trending markets, which are bullish or bearish, or nontrending markets, which trade within a bracketed high and low price range. However, once a market is in an established market type it stays there until it is played out. There are various technical and fundamental indicators that will reveal the approximate time and price at which a trending market will be exhausted and a reversal will take place.

Once a market establishes a trend, it is foolhardy for you, as an off-floor trader, to fade that trend. However, floor traders have always been able to scalp profits from incoming orders by fading the immediate trend. They have some important advantages over off-floor traders.

First of all, the pit trader has more liquidity in trade execution than an off-floor trader could ever have. When a floor trader fades a minor trend by selling contracts at the offered price, he has at his disposal the sell side orders coming into the pit to take him out of a bad trade. He will bid at the bid side, which will probably be under the last sale.

Let's look at an actual example of what a floor trader does: Assume that the market for Treasury bond futures is 90-15/32 bid and offered at 90-16/32. The high for the day is 90-15/32, so the market is moving up at the moment. The trend is short-term bullish. Orders to sell from the outside are coming in and finding buyers in the pit at 90-15/32, the high of the day. It is at this critical juncture of the trading scene that buy and sell orders are perfectly matched, with contracts changing hands at 90-15/32. The floor trader offers bonds at 90-16/32, which if transacted will be a new high price for the day. If the trader had bought at 90-14/32 just before the move to 90-15/32 bid and 90-15/32 offer, when the market action moved to a strong 90-15/32 bid with scattered offers at 90-15/32, he has inventory to sell at 90-16/32. If the strength of the intermediate trend is such that the market moves to 90-15/32 bid and 90-16/32 offered and transacted at the new high price of the day, market orders coming into the pit will be sold at whatever bids are represented in the pit: 90-15/32, and traders will sell out inventory at 90-16/32, giving them an immediate 1/32nd or 2/32nd profit. When the market moves to 90-16/32 bid and 90-17/32 offer, the trader who is short at 90-16/32 will be able to work the orders coming into the pit to sell at whatever the bid is.

Because they can sell at the offered price and buy at the bid price, pit traders can *appear* to trade against the trend and still make profits consistently. Outside traders, on the other hand, can only buy at the offer and sell at the bid price that the pit is currently trading at. They also have to pay a commission to enter the market. This means that there are two strikes against outside traders that will prevent them from trading against any short-term or intermediate trend. In order to overcome these two disadvantages, outside traders must trade with all odds in their favor. This can be done only by buying in a bull market and selling in a bear market. They cannot try to sell and buy like the floor traders who have a short-term frame of reference and an inherent commission advantage.

> *The strictest definition of a bull market is one in which prices move higher as time passes; in a bear market prices go lower as time passes.*

The strictest definition of a bull market is one in which prices move higher as time passes; in a bear market prices go lower as time passes. The velocity does not detract from the fact that prices will be moving in a trending direction.

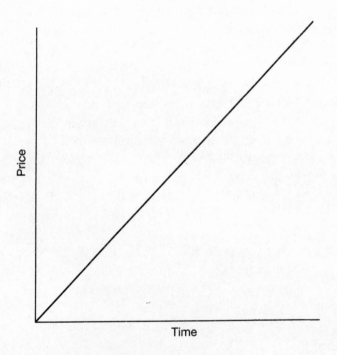

Fig. 7.1 A simplistic view of a bull market

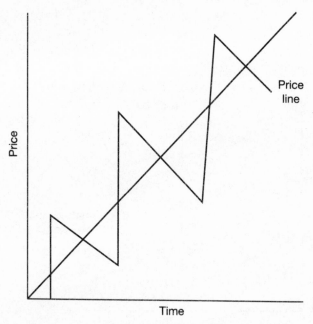

Fig. 7.2 A more detailed chart than Fig. 7.1, showing price line oscillating upward around the 45° line in a bull market

Figure 7.1 shows a line sloping upwards at a 45-degree angle. This illustration would be the most middle of the road example of an upward price slope. Prices, however, oscillate around this upward trendline, as shown in Figure 7.2. Figure 7.3 illustrates that the market can be oversold (OS), as shown by the troughs in the oscillating price trends, or overbought, as shown by the peaks in the oscillating price trends (OB).

If you look at the oscillating price movement in the bull trending illustration you can discern that every time price moves up two units, it only retraces one unit and never retraces more than two units. If a bull trend can be defined in such an oscillating fashion, then if you buy every time you have the chance to, your chances for a profit range from a probability of two to one in your favor at best (when oversold), to one to one at worst (when overbought). If you were to sell in a bull market every time you have the chance to, the odds at best would be one to one in your favor of making profits and one to two at worst against you. This type of ratio to profit play is open to every trader, yet most unsuccessful traders do not realize the impact of this little example.

31

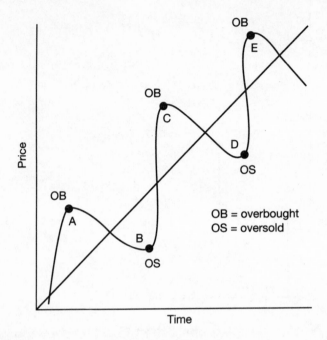

Fig. 7.3 A simplistic odds evaluation of the bull market

Situation 1: From Price Value A to B to C—Selling Short in a Bull Market.
If you sell in a bull market anywhere from point A to B, you have a maximum profit of one point (if you sell at A) and a minimum profit of zero points (if you sell at B). When price moves from B to C, your loss is two points when price reaches point C. If you sell at the best spot (point A), at C you have a one-point loss. If you sell at B, you have a two-point loss when price moves to C. If you sell at A and cover at B, you have the maximum profit of one point.

Situation 2: From Price Value A to B to C—Buying in a Bull Market.
If you buy instead of sell anywhere between points A and B, the results are dramatically different. If you buy at A and sell out at B, you lose a maximum of one point. If you buy at A and sell out at C, you make one point. If you buy at B, you could make a maximum of two points at price C.

Reverse the situation in bear markets and you will see that if you sold every time you had the opportunity you would automatically have the odds on your side all the time. And if you have the odds in your favor everytime you trade, the very fact that there are no supports in bear markets and no resistances in bull markets ensures that you will make money.

RULE 8

THE LONG-TERM TREND OF THE MARKET IS ALWAYS BULLISH BECAUSE THE LOSERS FADE AWAY

Markets are bullish, but not bullish enough for you and me to make much money in. What I've discovered about blatantly obvious statements such as these is that upon further investigation they really aren't that obvious. Just because the long-term averages go up doesn't mean that the average person will make any profits. The reason is more subtle than the average investor's ability to select profitable investments.

Several years ago I met one of the slickest salesmen in the commodity business I have had the bad fortune to ever know. This salesman had found a very slick way to give the impression that his buy and sell recommendations were always profitable. By accident he backed his way into an extremely profitable trading system. What happened to this salesman illustrates how his own impatience caused him to destroy his system.

In his promotional campaigns on the national finance station, FNN/CNBC cable television, he had created commercials offering his free newsletter. In this newsletter he made and then tracked his recommendations to buy and sell certain commodities.

He showed me his newsletter and was very proud of it. He pointed out the table that tracked the recommendations. I looked at the open trade profits and losses and was surprised that the profits were huge and the losses were small. I blurted out to him that he must have been doing something right to get these results.

He quietly told me the newsletter was one of his best marketing tools he had for selling his brokerage services. He designed the newsletter to be a promotional piece which showed huge profits and small losses.

As he was telling me this, I wondered to myself that it took me many years of hard-earned experience in the markets finally to be able to get to the point of being able to hang onto winners and cut my losers. Here was someone selling a trading methodology which racked up huge profits and small losses. He implied to me that he had absolute control of his market positions. He told me he cranked out these results every day with great ease!

As I engaged in further discussion with him, he revealed his little "secret" to me.

In a weak moment of revelation, he said, "Bill, there's nothing hard to learn about the system. Even though the system shows so well, I'm still losing money year after year."

Now I was even more puzzled. He continued, "What I do is this, Bill. After I've randomly picked out a market to get into, I put on the trade. The trade can then show a profit or it can show a loss. I guarantee you that in about three days, I will either have a $300 winner in that trade or a $300 loser. None of my losing trades stay on my books for more than three days. The winning trade I leave alone. As long as the open position shows a profit I don't close it out. Because I don't close it out, it shows up as open trade equity in my recommended commodities list. The closed trades no longer continue to show on the list and the losses from them are clumped together into one losing number. Meanwhile, I have these huge open trade profits. This looks real good to the prospective client."

I mused to myself that this salesman was doing exactly what a good trader should do: let his profits run and cut his losses. The irony was that the salesman didn't know what he had done. He had accidentally gotten himself into the only profitable trading and investing strategy that I know. For the wrong reason—he wanted to show huge profits and no open trade losses by removing the losers based on a three-day holding period—he was past the hardest part of trading (cutting losses and running with winners).

Playing devil's advocate, I asked him about the comparison of his current equity to starting capital. Surely the newsletter recipients would see that the capital was being drawn down due to market losses. He said the recipients seldom paid attention to those numbers. They were enthralled most of the time with the huge open profits! And, he told me, to track the drawdowns, the recipients must have more than two issues of the newsletter. Most only had one issue before they became this broker's clients. If they got two or more, the broker would have endeared himself to them already; by then, the prospective client was on a first-name basis with the broker.

> *The past ten years have been the most bullish in our 200-year history. In our own generation, anybody who bought stocks 10 years ago has made huge profits. In the rest of the past 200 years, the majority of stock owners have lost money on stock selection.*

He was losing money overall because his trade selections were pretty bad: He randomly picked trades. His percentage of winners to losers trade by trade probably was considerably less than 50 percent.

Meanwhile, his public record of open positions showed phenomenal profits, which razzled and dazzled the prospective clients. The markets are essentially what this salesman had lucked into.

How can the market be generally bullish when most of us who've ever invested in stocks have owned stocks which went lower after we bought them? What about all those turkeys? In fact, a lot of those stocks have gone sour. So how can anyone agree that the markets are generally bullish?

Let's look at how this is so. The stock market is presently composed of about 8,000 stocks in the United States. Not all of these stocks were trading ten years ago. And 20 years ago, not all those stocks were trading then either. This can be dragged further back to when the New York Stock Exchange was founded. Over the course of the market's history more stocks have disappeared or have not gone anywhere than have remained on the exchange; however, the current formulas to account for them do not incorporate these "failed" companies.

You get my point: every day more new stocks are traded. Tomorrow another handful of new stocks will be traded. Meanwhile, the stocks which have gone down and all which have gone bankrupt will be replaced by ones that go up, until even then the time comes for these latter arrival bullish stocks to go down themselves.

What happens to the stocks which go bad? What about the bankruptcies? Well, these stocks fall gracefully and eventually go to zero. Then they're removed from our consciousness.

Have you ever tried to find out what happened to one of your penny stocks which was last trading at 1 cent a share after a 50-cent selloff? I wish you luck! You will have better luck finding a stock certificate from these companies from collectors and dealers in stock certificates than from the transfer agents.

The bad stocks are like the commodities trades which show losses in three days for our salesman. They are removed, stricken from our thoughts and never to be mentioned again. This is as close as you will ever get to Darwinism of stocks.

The stocks that go from a small office machine company to IBM or from Haloid Corporation to Xerox Corporation, are the stocks that stick with us as time goes by. We hear and read about these stocks all the time. These upwardly mobile stocks stay in our consciousness for years because they are around for years.

Similar to our salesman's newsletter continued display of his commodity trades with his huge open trade profits, the stocks that are winners are on the books and are displayed to the public. They're listed in the financial pages everyday. Analysts are always writing reports about them. Stockbrokers are always promoting them. You can hardly find anybody working in the business who doesn't have a story about them.

No wonder the vast majority of stock players have shown losses while the rest of the world was truthfully observing the

Dow Jones Industrials and the S&P 500 making new historical highs. The past ten years have been the most bullish in our 200-year history. In the context of our own generation, anybody who bought stock 10 years ago has made huge profits. In the rest of the past 200 years, which are more "normal," the majority of stock owners have lost money on stock selection.

So the newsletter is just like the stock market—bullish in appearances only. Bullish in appearance only because the losers never hang around long enough after their demise to be factored into the equations. The winning stocks and commodities will continually be in the public eye.

The solution to mitigating your trading losses is to pick better markets to buy or sell. The solution is not to accept typical statements, such as markets have always gone up and you can't go wrong if you invest from a broad base from the long side in a historically "obviously" bullish trending market. Nothing is further from the truth.

Unlike the salesman who didn't know what he had stumbled onto, you are now aware that all you need to do is to pick better stocks for the right reasons. This means that you, as the owner of the portfolio of stocks, must toss out bad stocks in your portfolio, just as our salesman had done so with his bad recommendations. I wonder, as an aside, what the academics who have performed portfolio studies over the course of many years would obtain as total overall results if they had factored in all stocks traded, not just the ones that remain. The ones that get tossed out will have a dampening effect on overall bullishness of the markets. (Perhaps the investment return on stocks should then be equivalent to those of commodities since the bad stocks would not be eliminated, just as commodities price performance is always included in commodities returns.)

This also means you can't continue to believe that since the markets have gone up a majority of investors have been making money.

RULE 9

IF YOU DON'T KNOW WHAT'S GOING ON, DON'T DO ANYTHING

This elementary rule is so familiar to most traders that they give it lip service and dismiss it. But you would be surprised at how often traders get into situations that they have to nurse to profitability by doing exactly what this rule admonishes against.

The problem that most people who try to become successful traders have with this rule is that they will not perform the study that is necessary to make a successful trade until *after* the trade is made. By this time the trader is either nursing a position that is inherently unsound or else he takes profits way too early, both of which are terrible trading strategies.

To illustrate the importance of research, I will compare the mental and physical process of purchasing a household item to that of trading in the markets.

If you were buying a new VCR, for example, you would probably ask your friends for their advice about which brand to purchase and then compare the features of each model they recommend. To fortify your decision you might pick up a copy of some test reports to find out what was written about your choices. You would begin doing this weeks or months before you actually purchased a machine. When you were ready to buy, you would look for a sale at a local department store or check the prices in the advertisements in newspapers and magazines. You would then select the one that has the cheapest prices and the best guarantee protections. Finally, you would use it for about a week to see if it fulfilled your needs in a VCR. If you were unhappy with your purchase you would return it for a refund or a credit against another purchase. That's all there is to purchasing a VCR!

> *The problem that most people who try to become successful traders have with this rule is that they will not do the study that is necessary to make a successful trade until after the trade is made.*

Now let's see what goes on in a stock or futures transaction. Your commodities broker calls you at the office one morning and tells you of a developing situation in the cocoa markets caused by a boll weevil that has been destroying all the crops. Or, if it's your stockbroker, he tells you of the latest rumor on a major acquisition: General Motors, after having failed at bringing in H. Ross Perot to computerize it, is going to make a tender offer for IBM. You know that the profits you could make on either trade would pay for this year's vacation to the Bermudas. Still cautious, you tell your broker you'll think about it and get back to him tomorrow. As the day wears on, the thought of riding a market winner tempts you more. By the time you get home you know you will have to buy a couple of contracts, not just one. Next morning, your broker calls to remind you that the markets are going to open in 15 minutes. Deliberately and methodically he says to you, "Do you want to get on board this winning trade?" You swallow hard. The glowing bodies in the Club Med posters glow back at you. "Yeah, buy me five contracts on the opening." Done.

The first major difference between the VCR purchase and the stock or futures transaction is the time frame. In the case of the VCR, you had ample time to familiarize yourself with the product before making a purchase. In a stock or futures transaction you talk to your broker on the phone and within minutes you are the owner of five cocoa contracts. The broker tries to make it as easy as possible for you to execute trades. Nonetheless, it always seems that when you want fast execution of a trade, your broker's service is not fast enough, but when you need time for strategic consideration of a possible trade, time flies.

The second difference is a psychological one: the greed and fear associated with making money. When you buy a VCR, you actively solicit outside opinions, and people are generally willing to offer you their best advice. When you are buying stocks or futures, on the other hand, you will find that very few people are willing to impart information on how to make money. You yourself might be reluctant to talk about money matters with other people. Some people won't even talk about money with their spouse, yet good advice on trading and speculating is more critical than it is on the purchase of a VCR.

The third difference deals with the nature of the way products and risk vehicles are bought and sold. The VCR is returnable if you aren't happy with it. It's only a loss of your time if you decide to return it within a reasonable period. Stocks and futures contracts are not returnable if you aren't satisfied with your decision. Of course, if the stocks or futures appreciate in price while you are holding them, you stand to gain from that appreciation if you sell your interests to another buyer at the higher price. Why are risk vehicles sold on a no-return basis? Perhaps it is because stocks and futures were designed to be sold rather than bought.

RULE 10

TIPS DON'T MAKE
YOU ANY MONEY

Tips are pieces of information that come from questionable sources with no known way of tracing them.

It's not true that tips don't make you any money. Reliable tips can make good money for you. One trader had a tip on American Hospital Supply stock before it was taken over by Baxter Labs several years ago. In less than 24 hours he made $250,000. I've made money on reliable tips, but I've also lost money on tips that turned out bad.

The issue of using tips for profit goes beyond the issue of right or wrong, although tips do present an unfair advantage to investors and traders who are privy to such information. The real issue is the need to function as an independent, self contained trader. Unlike the role traders take when they actively pursue fundamental or technical research, the traders who seek tips are passive. Once traders relinquish their autonomy by relying on tips, they might as well start to work for someone else. They become, in a sense, employees of the tip giver.

As a long-term trader with a vested interest in the markets, it is better to make money by correctly analyzing the markets yourself. Then you become the master of your own destiny. As you learn to read market action, your skill in the markets is transportable. That is, you can take the knowledge that you have acquired and trade from anywhere in the world without having to rely on tips. Conceptually and practically, all markets behave in the same manner. Once you know how to trade successfully, you can transfer correct trading practices from one market to another with ease.

> **It is better to make money by correctly analyzing the markets yourself.**

On the other hand, if you learn to make money by relying on tips, you are no longer free to trade any market. You are dependent on your source, who in turn is dependent on his or her source, and so on, upwards to the ultimate source. The chain of tip givers must not be broken if you are to continue to make profits on tips. As an independent trader I find this situation confining.

In the realm of market analysis, the trader takes in all the information that he or she has access to in order to arrive at a decision to buy or sell particular markets. The type of information the trader inputs into his or her analysis falls into two types: technical data and fundamental data. These data are available to everyone, and the sources of the data are continuous and credible. Knowing how to read the data is a specialized skill that you learn and can implement in the market every day. Not so with reliance on tips.

The argument for using tips is that you can take one tip and ride it all the way to several hundred thousand dollars or millions of dollars of profits. However, in the process of making all these ill-gotten gains, you forget about doing anything else. You no longer try to apply fundamental or technical analysis to market situations. You no longer treat the market as a business.

Those who do get burned by tips are too embarrassed to talk about it and also are afraid to cut off the source of their tips, bad as they might be. Bad information from fundamental sources will eventually stop because of market forces. Traders will stop paying for such information. The same applies to bad technical analysis techniques. If a trading technique is flawed, market forces will shunt it aside in favor of better ones. The dynamics of tip giving and receiving are not subject to the natural selection process of the marketplace. Good tips are given to only a few. Bad tips are given to everyone.

The next time you hear a tip, check the source. It might be a distribution of stocks or futures by the tipsters.

RULE 11

USE THE RIGHT ORDERS TO GET INTO THE MARKETS ·

There are many types of orders that you can give your broker to execute, depending on what you want to do and how you want to do it. You must use the right type of order to get the right results.

Most of my orders are market orders. If I want to get into a position, I enter a market order at the prevailing price. Conversely, if I want to liquidate my position, I do it at the market. My feeling has always been to get a position in the market: If bullish, I want to own something, and if bearish, I want to sell something.

Most traders do not like to execute their orders at the market price but at a limit price. These traders are really saying that the likely market scenario, either continuation of a bullish or bearish move, won't occur until their price limit is reached. This type of thinking implies that the market will act according to the trader's wishes. This is patently absurd. The market will do what it wants to do. It is the role of the trader to figure out what the markets are doing in order to profit from them.

There are times when orders other than market orders are not only preferred, but required for good trade execution. The following are the most common types of orders and the market conditions under which they may be used.

Limit orders

These orders specify execution at a certain price limit. A buy limit order would direct the executing broker to buy at a specified

43

price limit. A sell limit order specifies the price at which an issue should be sold. If the price of the issue is currently at $24 and you

> *There are times when orders other than market orders are not only preferred, but required for good trade execution.*

tell a broker that you want to buy a certain amount at $22, your broker will not try to execute the order unless it first reaches $22, and you won't be guaranteed an execution until it goes below $22. The converse is true in bull markets where you enter orders to sell at a fixed price greater than the current market price.

Limit orders are like trading blindfolded. If the price of a stock is at $24, but you feel that $22 is a fairer price, then this is not the right time to buy it. If you give a limit order to your broker to buy it at $22, you're saying that you won't be around to watch the stock go to $22 but want your broker to represent you when it reaches that price. If it goes to $22 when you're not watching it, what makes you think that the conditions that were present when the stock was at $24 did not change to new conditions that might make the stock a less attractive purchase at the lower price of $22? In short, when you tell your broker to buy or sell something at a price that is not at the current market, you're telling him to execute your trade and ignore whatever new reasons there might be to explain why the price has changed.

Market-if-touched (MIT)

An MIT order is executed at the prevailing market price when a price limit that you determined ahead of time is reached. This is to differentiate it from the limit order, which is executed at a fixed price once that price is reached. Market-if-touched orders are used in markets that swing from liquidity to illiquidity. The price action will encounter pockets of extreme to moderate activity, depending on where prices are at the time. Implied in an MIT order is that once your limit is reached, you want your order to be filled at any price. You don't want to hang around with your order until another price level is reached.

I have often used MIT orders in the bond futures market closes. The last 15 minutes of trading are often hectic if the futures start to trade strongly in one direction. Before the last quarter hour I look at the high or low of the day and enter an MIT order just slightly above either side of the range. If I am long and want to liquidate the long, I enter an MIT order several ticks above the high of the day if the market appears to be ready to charge into new high territory. If the market has enough strength to punch through new highs at the last quarter hour of trading, it often represents some sort of hectic rush to buy, perhaps a panic short covering rally. I want my order to be offered at the market once the limit is reached so that I can squeeze a few extra ticks out of it. It's not surprising to see the price jump by two to three ticks under such closing price conditions. The alternative is to wait until a few minutes before the close time and rush in a market order; this approach puts too much pressure on the phone clerks and the executing broker on the floor. I like to ease the task of the order takers so that they don't make mistakes that I often have to pay for.

Contingency orders

These are composites of two different types of orders based on sympathetic markets that follow the movements of other markets: Silver follows gold, the Dow Jones industrials follows the Dow Jones transportations, wheat futures follow oat futures, etc. When a limit price or a certain market condition is reached on the first order, the second order is executed. Most exchanges do not allow such orders, but you can create a hybrid order if you can get your broker to handle it.

To illustrate how a contingency order is created let's take a look at orders to buy silver futures based on the strength of gold prices. Your broker tracks the price of gold. Once a gold price limit is reached, he goes to the second part of your order and attempts to execute the order to buy silver. Your order might read: "Buy five February delivery month of silver futures at the market contingenton May delivery month of gold futures reaching $420." If the gold futures trade at $420 or above after your order is entered, then it is incumbent on the retail broker to send an order into the silver pit to buy your five contracts. If a floor broker is willing to accept the order, the floor broker in the silver pit will be executing the order and monitoring the gold prices. Most floor brokers are too busy to handle such orders, but retail brokers can generally take this order because they have the price monitoring equipment available. Of course, don't expect your retail broker to monitor the prices of both markets in order to execute such an order.

I seldom use contingency orders because they are very messy to follow and track. If there is a mistake on the execution, it is difficult to obtain times and sale prices to support any arguments. Why bother when it's so much easier to enter your positions at the market?

One cancels the other

This is a real strange order. Again, there are two types of orders involved here. It's also a contingency order where if either the first or the second order's conditions are met, then the remaining order, the second or the first, is canceled.

I have used these orders to buy or sell a futures contract when I had no preference on the delivery month. If the first two delivery months are trading freely, I enter an order to buy either the first one if its price is reached or the second one if its price is reached. Once one order is executed, the other is canceled. I have never had both orders filled at the same time because there is only one executing broker for this type of order. If two brokers in two different markets were executing the order, then it is possible that both orders could be filled, but no broker would take such an order because he or she would be forced to rely on another broker for an execution.

Fill or kill (FOK)

I used to use this type of order until I realized that it doesn't give any better fills and only aggravates the traders and market makers. The order is entered into the trading pit or to the specialist like any other order, except that all the conditions of the order have to be met or else it is cancelled, or killed. There is no such thing as a partial fill or a fill at varying prices. An FOK order could read: "Buy 30 January soybeans at $5.60, fill or kill." The executing floor broker offers to buy all 30 contracts at $5.60, and will not accept 10 contract sat $5.55,10 at $5.60, and 10 at $5.65 for an average price of 30 at $5.60. Fill or kill orders have been used because some traders who want an execution right then and there will enter the fill or kill component to the order because of slow reporting procedures. I also did that until my broker caught on to what I was doing.

When you decide to enter the market, your role is to put on a position in the market, not to mastermind how you will obtain your order. A market order is the best way to obtain a position in the market. There are rare occasions under which you can use other orders, more in the areas of exiting your trades than in entering your trades. If you have to be fancy about entering orders, use a market order to enter your position and use the other orders to exit.

RULE 12

Don't Be Whimsical About Closing Out Your Trades

Traders spend a good portion of their waking hours analyzing the markets. They try to determine how they can enter the markets correctly, yet they spend very little time planning what to do if their analysis is wrong. They also don't predetermine points where they can take profits.

Initiating a trade is only one part of the total process. There are really three parts to a trade: (1) decision making, (2) execution, and (3) management. Each part is critical to successful trading, and each part must follow in sequence. However, the only part that makes money is the management part.

The first part of the trade is decision making. Most traders learn techniques of fundamental and technical analysis to help them decide whether they should go long or short in a trade. It takes a long time to gain knowledge in this area, and the learning curve is steep. Hence, this part of the trade makes no money for the trader.

In fundamental analysis the trader analyzes the balance sheets and income statements of companies to predict future price movements of the stocks. The analyst tries to predict future trends in past assets, earnings, sales, products, management, markets, and other indicators. He or she assesses whether a particular stock or group of stocks is undervalued or overvalued at the current market price. The fundamentalist analyzes commodities, interest rates, and foreign currencies with these tools.

The technical analyst, on the other hand, looks at supply and demand in terms of price, time, and volume action. The analyst tries to discover repeatable patterns by charting these types of data. Once the analyst classifies price, time, or volume action into repeatable patterns, he or she can then forecast future patterns.

Traders cannot learn fundamental or technical analysis overnight. From my own experience, it takes several years to become proficient with these tools. The times spent learning the analytical tools causes many traders to over emphasize this portion of a trade.

The second part of a trade is the execution. Although this part of the trade can be learned within a month, it also does not make the trader any money; at best, it will reduce price skids on trades. After the trader has decided to either buy or sell, there is a spectrum of approaches to executing the trade. The trader can enter a trade at the market price or at a limit price; he can enter a long position with a stop buy order or a short position with a stop sell order; he can close out a position at the market with a stop on the close only; he can place contingency orders; he can buy at noon and sell 15 minutes before the close, etc.

Sometimes traders confuse the decision-making tools with the trade execution tools and begin to view the execution part of the trade to be the same as the decision-making part. These traders end up trading more often than they should and for much less profit than they can get.

The third part of the trade is the management of the position. This part makes all the money. It is the most critical part of a *successful* trade. Successful traders handle this part well. Unsuccessful traders are unaware that this portion of a trade exists.

When the trade turns into a profit, the unsuccessful trader takes his profits; the winning trader tries to determine whether or not the trade will continue to show more profits. If it shows promise of more profits, the trader allows it to run its course.

Losing trades don't start as large losses, but as controllable small losses. When unsuccessful traders have a small loss, they allow it to expand. If they want to move into the winners' class, they must learn to manage their trades correctly.

49

Of the three parts of a trade, position management requires the least amount of study, for there is nothing to study, yet it is the only part that can make the profit. The part that does require study is the study of yourself and your own personality traits. You must know how comfortable you are with yourself as a winner, how you cope with failure, and how you handle disagreements in life.

> *Of the three parts of a trade, position management requires the least amount of study, for there is nothing to study, yet it is the only part that can make the profit.*

It is difficult not to lump the three parts of a trade together because the decision-making process takes the longest time to learn. However, a trader who becomes consumed by the act of deciding doesn't know what to do with the trade once it is executed. If the decision to enter the trade is incorrect, the trader does not know how to get out and allows the losses to compound. If the decision to enter the trade is correct, the trader does not know how to manage the position. He or she sells out too soon and prevents the profits from accruing.

When you learn the process of making a trade over several years, the three parts to a trade appear to overlap to the point where you cannot see their demarcations.The next time you want to make a trade, decide what you want to do based on fundamental analysis, technical analysis, or a combination; then execute the trade. Finally, bring out your desire to make a profit: Manage the position correctly. Remember that when you start a trade, you are only partially on the way on the road to wealth!

RULE 13

WITHDRAW A PORTION OF
YOUR PROFITS

The business of trading is very profitable when you know what to do in the markets. Unlike other businesses, when you don't know what you are doing in the trading business, your losses are unlimited and can come along rapidly. In other businesses when you don't know what you are doing you can buy talent to mitigate the losses. In trading, you have only yourself to rely upon.

Because they have learned to rely on themselves, traders have rather large egos, especially after successfully completing a trading campaign. We need to reward ourselves for doing well in the markets, but the rewards must be translated into tangible things. Money in a trading account is not a tangible item. Buy yourself nice clothes, take a well-deserved vacation, or buy a new car.

What you mustn't do is to reward yourself by taking bigger market risks. When you do make money trading, you must take a portion of the profits out and put it in a separate account. This is an absolute requirement for your long-term stability in the business. The role of a professional speculator is to reduce trading risks in market positions, even to the point of limiting the capital that they have in their trading accounts.

I can hear a reader saying, "When I have the money in my account, I can take on bigger positions so that I can make the million dollar trades." This is a valid thought. However, please note that I suggest that you take out a *portion* of your profits, not all of your profits. In this manner, you will still have a portion of your profits to trade increasingly larger positions following successful trades. With this cautiously risk-reducing attitude towards profits, you'll have money to spend if you're unlucky enough to run through a series of bad trades.

> *One of the best investments that one can make with the profits is to take long, relaxing vacations. Most unsuccessful traders will take vacations when they can least afford them: when they have just been nailed in the markets.*

The bottom line to making more money in the markets is to increase trading size, but this must be coupled with good market analysis. Some unsuccessful traders mistakenly believe that they can avoid increasing trading size by merely increasing frequency. (When I see floor traders suddenly jump from low activity to high activity, they are probably in trouble with their positions.) Every time a trader has a position in the marketplace, there is always risk. The only way to have no risk is to have no positions. As an aside to what is the correct way to increase your trading position, I have several thoughts.

When you initiate longs at the beginning of a bull move you trade the number of positions that your account can handle; however, you're always wondering when the position will turn into a profit so that you can parlay that profit into more positions. For whatever the reasons, we find ourselves sticking profits into our trading account so that we can accumulate more positions on the long side. At the beginning and bottom of the move we are long one contract. At the top of the move, with its inevitable reversal, we are long 50 contracts. As the market gets closer to the top, we should be long only one contract. And at the beginning and bottom of the move we should be long 50 contracts.

One of the best investments that one can make with the profits is to take long, relaxing vacations. The irony of this business is that most unsuccessful traders will take vacations when they can least afford them: i.e., when they have just been nailed in the markets. After losing a bundle in the markets, some traders will dig into their trading account for a few thousand dollars to pay for a trip to club Med or the Bahamas. After losing such an amount, they are more than willing to be away from trading, although this further depletes their trading capital. Had the partial profits been taken out when there were some, the losing traders could have tapped this reserve fund without having to go into their trading account for more money. As you will see in other chapters, the psychology of separating types of funds to trade with, types of funds to invest with, and types of funds to pay living expenses with, etc., affect you as a trader. Capital that is stashed away somewhere where it cannot be touched by an adverse market move gives the trader confidence to weather bad market situations.

Some traders reward themselves on both the tangible level and the risk level: They take the long vacation or buy the expensive sports car, and they also take the bigger trading risks. This is a very bad way to approach the investment of one's profits. The cost for the long vacation or the car is a one-time expense, but the risk of trading capital can be recurring. How many times have we heard of traders who can't afford to trade any more because they took a hit in the markets? Had they stashed away their investments and capital, they would have had reserves to fall back on.

If you make $2,000 profits in a $10,000 trading account, you have made a 20 percent return on your total risk capital. If you continue to trade and view your total risk capital as $12,000, you have increased the amount of your risk capital to 120 percent of your original $10,000. On the other hand, if you had withdrawn half of you trading profits, $1,000, you would have $11,000 to continue to trade with, and $1,000 stashed away or invested. You will be surprised at how good it feels to have that $1,000 stashed away.

A good rule of thumb is to withdraw half of your profits out of your trading account every month and completely ignore the amount withdrawn. Consider only how much is in your trading account as the risk capital. If you follow this rule, you will be able to consistently make money from the markets instead of consistently contributing to the health and wealth of other traders.

One trader I know always takes out a portion of his profits every month. One month he pulled out enough profits to buy a cabin in Wisconsin. Another month he pulled out profits to buy a racing boat. He doesn't follow the percentage rule strictly, but he pulls out a portion of his profits on a consistent basis. The last six months, the markets have been dull and he hasn't had the profits to pull out. But he does have the cabin in Wisconsin and his racing boat to help him patiently wait out the next market moves. He isn't forced to push the markets for moves that aren't there. If he hadn't invested part of his profits in this manner, he would have taken a few shots here and there, increasing his chances of losing money by trying to force the markets to make money for him when it isn't possible.

RULE 14

DON'T BUY A STOCK ONLY TO OBTAIN A DIVIDEND

This chapter could be titled "Be Careful of Inducements Offered to Purchase a Stock, Especially Dividends." There are so many ways the marketers of stocks make their product more attractive to prospective purchasers that a whole book on marketing the stock market would be the only way to do the subject justice.

The public investor perceives that one of the reasons for stock ownership is the return on an investment. This can be as simple as the quarterly dividend paid out to holders of the stock or as complicated as factoring in the profits accrued from a covered write into the capital gains of the underlying stock. In the former case, the dividend is issued from the company itself. In the latter, additional profits are accumulated through the investor's own acumen.

I personally would rather rely on the investor's own acumen. I've never heard of any company management who consistently did anything for the strict benefit of the stockholders. For all practical purposes, ownership of the working operations of companies is never transferred to stockholders because their ownership is fragmented. Stockholder control can be implemented through the accumulation of enough voting rights, but getting enough stockholders together to make their voting rights count is tantamount to a complete reorganization of the company. Management still owns the right to control the destiny of the company.

The stock market is more complex than the futures markets or other capital markets because of the inducements that make them appealing to various groups of prospective purchasers. In the futures markets, the appeal to prospective purchasers is broken down into two aspects of an equation: supply and demand.

> *Woe to the investor who buys a stock because of a dividend increase and finds that the dividend is later canceled!*

In the stock markets, there are many different groups of potential buyers: people who buy stocks because they want to have capital gains; people who buy stocks because some interesting news captured their interest; people who buy stocks to take advantage of arbitrage plays; and people who buy stocks to obtain dividends. Each group can be lured into the marketing of stocks at different entry points in the cycle. These people with diverse interests can be further broken down into two categories: capital gains players and return on investment players.

Let's analyze the creation of stock for the purpose of making it available on the open market. Once you see how the markets are structured you will see how dividends enter into the game of marketing stocks. There are several important facts to realize about the marketing of stocks: Who is selling the stock, and who is buying it? If you owned a privately held company and you were selling some or all of your company to someone else, would you sell your company at bargain prices or would you try to get the best possible price for it?

Marketing has to be implemented by the owners. They have interests in the company, and they would like to convert that ownership to cash. The cleverest owners also are able to retain absolute control of the companies they once owned but now manage "on behalf of the stockholders": They use the assets of the company and the assets of the new shareholders to enrich themselves.

Like retail advertising, stock marketing has a language of its own. Instead of saying "comparable to a higher priced item," which a department store would say to sell its refrigerators, the stock marketer says "now selling at a fraction of its all-time high." Take a look at the following list of comparable marketing messages.

Department Store	Stock Marketer
New and improved	New oil discoveries
Guaranteed to enhance your life	Looks like another Xerox
Inventory clean-up	Quarterly house cleaning
Buy one, get one free	Stock split
Heavy duty	Blue-chip defensive issue
High-quality at a value price	AAA rating with high return
Incredibly new	New issues with potentials
Sensational savings	An insider buying chance
Extra-strength	Overbought
Last call for savings	Challenging former highs
More for less	Hard asset play
Extra nutrition	Undervalued assets
Nothing protects better	Virtually no downside
Ouchless	No margin calls
100% natural	No market makers in this
No preservatives	No strings attached
Clinically tested mild	Research analysts recommend
Easy to use—no mess	Just sign the account forms
We sell excitement	Glamour stock situation
Less fat	Turnaround situation
Compare and save	Buy the leading issue

An investor who realizes that stocks are products to be marketed develops a healthy skepticism about the "advertising" that goes on in marketing the stocks. The wise investor knows how to read between the lines.

It should come as no surprise to readers that stocks are sold initially at very dear prices, just as department store products are marked up for sale to the customers. The founding owners of a company sell stocks of ownership at very high prices. Shortly after this point, bargains for the company's stock are available. There are exceptions, such as the new issues of Apple Computer, but for the most part stocks can be bought cheaper after the initial offering.

Bargains for stocks exist in one of two ways or a combination of the two: current owners, be they the founders or mere shareholders, unload stocks at below liquidation prices, or the company improves and grows while the stock price fails to respond to the fundamental changes.

It is a bad investment to buy stocks at above valuation prices, or at over valuation, at any stage of the marketing cycle. This gives you less potential for profits because the upside price moves would be limited. There are many ways that the stock marketer will make it easy for you to believe that the current over valuation of the price is justified, when it isn't the case.

Increasing a dividend on a stock is a mechanical way of making a stock more appealing for prospective investors. These prospects, however, are also sensitive to obtaining a rate of return for their investments. If accompany increases a dividend, it can just as easily decrease it. However, investors who are looking for returns on capital can mistakenly assume that once a dividend is declared the dividend payments will continue. Woe to the investor who buys a stock because of a dividend increase and finds that the dividend is later canceled!

RULE 15

Dollar Cost Averaging Works Best With Stocks That Fluctuate Widely; If the Stock is Not Always in a Declining Trend, You Should Come Out Ahead

The concept is based on frequently and consistently acquiring a stock over the life of an investment program with a fixed amount of capital each time. If you implement the plan, you buy a fixed dollar amount of stock, lets say $1,000 worth of IBM stock every month for the next 20 years. Over the life of the program you would have had the opportunity to pick up the stock at high prices and at low prices. At high prices you buy fewer shares, as it should be, and at lower prices you buy more shares, as it should be.

Figure 15.1 shows an example of dollar cost averaging at work. Note how the price of the particular stock in this example moves in two swings: one upward from $10 to $50, and one downward from $40 to $10. When the price moves upward, the profits are continual, but when the stock starts to move down the profits diminish rapidly and eventually the investor winds up holding positions with an average price considerably higher than the current market price. At the last addition of $10 for the

Stock's Price at End of Month	Invest $1,000 Each Month	Cumulative Stock Position	Total Out of Pocket Cost	Cumulative Market Value	Profit or Loss
$10	100 shares	100 shares	$1,000	$ 1,000.00	$ 0.00
15	66.67 shares	166.67	2,000	2,500.00	500.00
25	40 shares	206.67	3,000	5,166.75	2,166.75
30	33.33	240	4,000	7,200.00	3,200.00
35	28.57	268.57	5,000	9399.99	4,399.99
40	25	293.57	6,000	11,742.80	5,742.50
35	28.57	322.14	7,000	11,274.90	4,274.90
30	33.33	355.47	8,000	10,654.10	2,664.30
25	40	395.47	9,000	9,885.75	886.75
15	66.67	462.14	10,000	6,932.10	-3067.90
10	100	562.14	11,000	5,621.40	-5,378.60

Figure 15.1 Example of dollar cost averaging

100 shares, the average price of the total position, before the final addition is 462.14 shares with $10,000 invested, or an average price of $21.64 per share. After the addition of the 100 shares at $10, the total position is now $562.14 for an average price of $19.56. So, the investor has managed to reduce his or her average position's price by $21.64 minus $19.56, or $2.07 a share. Looking at this another way, the investor put up another $1,000 to reduce his total position's cost by $2.07 a share. Is this good or bad? Neither since this approach takes a long-term perspective. Implied is the belief that when the stock dips down to $10 the second time around the price will eventually go back up, beyond the now average position price of $19.56. It violates a lot of trading rules and strategies, such as "never add to a losing position and put stop orders to protect profits," but the reader can implement these rules and strategies personally into this dollar cost averaging scenario and improve the plan tremendously.

> *When diversifying in this program, make that sure the companies you have picked are not interrelated. Dollar cost averaging a portfolio of five companies over the life of 20 years when these companies are centered in one industry is not diversifying.*

This is a very basic approach and works well. However, it is also simplistic and negates the need to constantly monitor the fundamental and technical activities of the investment product. So, I have two suggestions to make this approach more effective.

First, find stocks that have a high probability of being around 20 years from now. These stocks are leaders in their industries and have a record over the last 20 years of expanding and paying out dividends. An ideal stock would be a growth stock that develops and then as it matures it takes its profits and proffers dividends to stockholders. You might want to consider this method for a core holding of stocks; this core holding makes up a good portion of your investment funds. Nothing is worse than owning a stock through the dollar cost averaging method and watching the stock go bankrupt.

The second point is to diversify your risk with this strategy by purchasing more than one company's stock. A reasonable number would be five quality stocks. With the fact that these companies are quality stocks, i.e., will be around 20 years from now, having five such companies will mitigate disastrous bankruptcies.

When diversifying in this program, make sure that the companies you have picked for your program are not interrelated. Dollar cost averaging a portfolio of five companies over the life of 20 years when these companies are centered in one industry is not diversifying. A good mix would be to pick a computer stock, telecommunication stock, transportation stock, food stock, and entertainment stock.

Each of these industries move in different bottoming and topping cycles. They don't have correlated cycles. When one is up the others will be down. With the one that's up, you buy less stock; with the one that's down, you buy more stock. With the paper profits on the one that's up, you offset the paper losses on the ones that are down.

Over the life of this program you will create a portfolio of stocks which will pay out a good dividend and will continue to grow. A subtler benefit of this approach is that this is a forced savings plan with the savings going into a stable group of stocks.

RULE 16

DON'T AVERAGE YOUR LOSSES

How many times have you had a position go against you? You planned the trade correctly, but soon after you bought your initial position, you discovered that the price you paid was higher than what it was now worth. The first trade was a loser compared to market price.

What could you do with this losing trade? You could sell it out and look to buy something else, or you could buy a few more shares or contracts at the now lower price. Which is the better solution to your dilemma? In most cases, I would suggest that you either cut your losses by selling out your position or else stay with the losing position.

Most people, however, would buy more at lower prices. They would average their losses on the way down if they are buying, or average their losses on the way up if they are shorting. There's an old saying that if it looked good at a higher price, it looks a lot better at a bargain price. This approach can work at times, but usually it won't. Traders determine whether they will average or not by looking at what they are trading: stocks, options, or futures. Let's look at each of these trading vehicles in terms of averaging losses.

When dealing with *stocks*, averaging losses at lower prices can often work, depending on the viability of the company you are averaging your position in. This means that the company you are buying mustn't go bankrupt or in any way destroy your ownership interest. If there is even a slight chance that your stock will become worthless through bankruptcy, you will never get back your investment.

If another company buys or merges with your company, the acquiring company either converts your ownership to a portion of the new company or pays you cash. You will have to average your losses in the newly formed company or else you will be cashed out and will realize a loss on your holdings in the original company. Investors who average their losses will do whatever they can to avoid this. After incurring forced losses due to mergers or buyouts, these investors will forsake their original plan to average their losses and will take the tendered cash to buy stock in the new company or to invest in other companies.

If you are averaging your losses in *options*, you must realize that this trading instrument has a decaying market value. It is best not to average on the buy side because if you are buying options, you will be adding to a position that will expire worthless. The intrinsic value of the option is based on how much the option is in-the-money. How much remains after the decay in the time value of the option? You won't have a chance to hang on to your position.

On the short side, you can sell options naked. If the position goes against you, you can sell more options, expecting that expiration will reduce your liability. However, not all options situations can be handled this way; you must evaluate each one separately. Suffice it to say that selling options that are going against you requires both intestinal fortitude and deep trading pockets to sustain the losses.

When I traded equity options at the Chicago Board Options Exchange, I knew a trader named Mort Miller, whose predominant strategy was selling strangles and straddles. For some years, underlying stocks gradually moved either up or down—the key word here is *gradually*. The decay in option premium over time made Mort a lot of money.

Mort called me aside one day in early 1987 and asked me to help him out. He told me he was just recuperating from a heart attack and couldn't seem to do anything right in the markets. The markets of 1986–1987 had moved straight up, which meant that one side of Mort's strangles always decayed in value while the other side always amounted to huge losses. For a while Mort continued to sell more options to average his losses on the side that appreciated in value. But as the market started to slow down, the short positions he had averaged his losses on would eventually decay to zero worth.

If he had only looked at the condition and stage of the stock markets, he would have realized that selling straddles and strangles was no longer profitable. In our discussion, Mort and I agreed on one thing: If you have enough money in your account, you can always average your positions in options by selling more options. The key words here are *if you have enough money in your account*. All you have to do is wait until expiration to force your

> *You often don't know that you have averaged your losses until it's too late because of the many subtleties involving the number and timing of your contracts.*

total short position to zero value. That early portion of 1987 was enough for Mort to put all his capital to test in the markets.

When averaging your losses in *commodities*, remember that commodities will always have some market value. Soybeans and grains will always have some value. Unlike stocks, if you average commodities, you do not have to worry that the price of your investment will go down to zero. What you do have to consider is the expiration of your contracts. The markets will force you to take physical delivery of your commodities, so you must have a lot of money. Average good faith deposits amount to about 10 percent of the market value of the contract. This barely covers your positions if you have sustained losses in your account while averaging your losses. The margin clerk will ask you to come up with the other 90 percent of your original contracts' total value.

When they trade in commodities, most investors and speculators rarely consider that they are playing these markets at a fraction of the total value of the contracts. Unfortunately, when it's time to take delivery of these commodities, most under capitalized players, up against the trading giants, will not be able to ante up.

In each of the three cases, stocks, options, or commodities, the initial consideration in averaging losses was whether or not the total investment or speculation could possibly disappear to zero value. With stocks, this was possible only if the company went bankrupt. With options, you could possibly average your losses only if you were a naked seller. Even with the zero-value consideration in mind, it would be rather risky. Though commodities always have intrinsic worth, it is extremely unlikely that the traders who speculate and try to average their losses would have enough capital to take physical delivery of the commodities at expiration.

Few players have the capital strength to take physical delivery of commodities. Those who do can make some interesting plays. I learned of one profitable risk-free interest rate play from a founder of a national television broadcasting firm. He was a speculator in silver and gold futures contracts at the New York Commodity Exchange and the London Metals Exchange.

The play was basically an arbitrage. When prices got too high in either New York or London, relative to the other exchange, he would sell those contracts and buy the undervalued contract. He would factor the cost of carrying the metals based on interest rates at the time. He would take physical delivery if the profits were there. With metals, physical delivery was the exception rather than the rule. Producers of the metals would have their holdings on deposit in the vaults of one of the exchanges. When traders made delivery, a certificate changed hands from seller to buyer; hence, there was no real physical movement of the metals. This arbitrage play was only available to speculators of his size, with the capital to take delivery of the metals and hold on to them while waiting for the hedged side of the transaction to be delivered at expiration. He was consistently able to make a 4 percent or better rate of return over the risk-free, 90-day T-bill rate. Unfortunately most such plays are not possible for the average speculator.

You often don't know that you have averaged your losses until it's too late because of the many subtleties involving the number and timing of your contracts. First, you must establish your contract size. How many contracts do you trade when you begin? If you commit to buy one contract, there is no need to average. You don't have to buy more either in the direction of the market in your favor or against the market. If you trade more than one contract at a time, then you can and should average your position. If you are a 50-lot trader, you can buy all 50 at a single price or you can ease yourself in at several different prices.

Let's say that you want to buy a position on a particular day because some of your indicators point to a valid buy area. If you buy part of your position at one price, you then have the option of spreading out the balance over many prices. If you average the balance of your total trading position at lower prices, does this mean that you are averaging your losses? Technically speaking, I would say yes. However, from the perspective of your whole trading strategy, you have established an average price for your total commitment in relation to the current market. If you were to add another sized contract the next day at a lower price away from the average of your first commitment or at a different time interval that same day, then I would say that you were averaging your losses. Be sure to make this subtle, but very critical, distinction.

Another point to keep in mind is the major difference between averaging your losses and pyramiding your position. In averaging your losses, you are acquiring more positions when prices are going against the intermediate trend. In pyramiding, you are adding to your position in the direction of the intermediate trend. I will discuss pyramiding extensively in Rule 24.

Another form of averaging losses entails selling another option month or contract to spread off risk. This is done every day in exchange trading pits. It simply requires the trader to concentrate buying in one option, commodity month, or stock and selling in another option, commodity month, or stock.

As an example, a trader concentrates on buying the January soybeans contracts, averaging his losses. He maintains knowledge of the bid and ask of the next commodity month, the May soybeans contracts. (Here, we also talk about the carrying charge markets versus non-carrying charge markets.) As the trader maintains and adds to his inventory of January soybeans contracts at whatever prices, he offers May soybeans at the offered price. If an order that bids up the May soybeans comes into the exchange pit, the trader will find himself locked into a spread position. He is long the January soybeans and short the May soybeans. The soybean market is a carrying charge market, hence defined factors, rather than random market movements, go into the cost of carrying the soybeans from January to May. The difference in price between January and May soybeans is stable. The trader reverses the process when he takes profits. He bids for the May soybeans by averaging down and offers the January soybeans at the offering price. Spreading off averaged positions is viable only if the commission costs are negligible, and even then, the trader is working on razor thin profits in very liquid markets. I don't suggest that the upstairs trader do this type of trading.

Although this strategy of spreading off averaged positions works best in carrying charge markets, it is also used in non-carrying charge markets such as the meats traded at the Chicago Mercantile Exchange. The trader must be fully aware that the difference in price from one delivery month to another is never stable. This instability of price relationships merely adds to the riskiness of this strategy. Instead of dealing in only one contract month, the spread trader in such markets brings in the tentativeness of an unstable spread risk.

If you have been following my train of thought up to this point, you are probably wondering how you can make big money in the markets with only a small winning position. It's fine to be right on a five lot in the Treasury bond futures, but it's better to be able to add to your position and be long 50 contracts for a price move in your favor. Well, the correct way to add to your position is not by averaging your losses. By doing so, you are buying in the opposite direction of a market's intermediate move. Start on a very conservative basis for your first commitment. Ride the position to the top and then take profits. On the next move up, increase your initial commitment. For example, in the first go-around you buy 10 bonds and watch it go up. You take profits and either short or get out of the market completely. When the bonds bottom out, you then buy 20 bonds as an initial commitment. You ride this bond commitment to the top and then sell out. When you are able to do this again and again, you will increase your size to the point that a move can mean hundreds of thousands of dollars to you. This strategy will limit your losses to only a fraction of your total trading commitment.

RULE 17

Take Big Profits and Small Losses

We have read this rule many times, yet many people don't really understand it. If we did, most of us would have profits in our trading accounts instead of losses.

If you are an off-floor trader, the first obstacle to following this rule is your broker. A broker's profits are not based on what you make, but on the number of transactions you have going in your account. If your broker executes your trade and it is an immediate loser, he or she will tell you to wait out the trade so that you can get back to even. This is a bad approach because I have found that the first loss is usually the smallest. Unknowingly, your broker can cause your losing position, which started out as a small loss, to become a larger loss. The broker says that the loss will be made up over time, but how do you know that the markets will accommodate you?

If the trade shows a profit, your broker will be the first to tell you that "You will never go broke taking a profit." This is true, but this is not the way to make big money. Profits, when you are able to cash out of them, mean that your account has increased in size, but this is only part of the profit-making equation. If all your losses are as big, dollarwise, as your wins, there is some justification for ringing the cash register every time you can; but most traders and investors find that their losses are bigger than their profits on a per trade basis. Because of this imbalance, I try to squeeze whatever I can out of a profitable trade.

When taking profits I use a strategy that is based on simple logic. If the position shows a profit immediately, I unload part of the position. That is, if I am showing profits on 400 shares of stocks or 40 futures contracts, I can ring the register by selling half the position. Depending on how badly I want to get rid of my profitable positions and how comfortable I feel with the actual position, I vary the percentage I sell, but I never sell the full position. I have discovered that when I do have a profitable position on and I am trading correctly with the market trend, I make substantially more money on the balance of my position than I did on the part that I sold.

> *When taking profits I use a strategy that is based on simple logic. If the position shows a profit immediately, I unload part of the position.*

If you have to do something to an existing position that is showing a profit, you can add on to it. Selling out a profitable position is a tendency in human nature that will prevent you from ever making any substantial profits. It is better to buy more instead of selling out your position totally. If you can't do this, then sell out only part of the position.

The caveat here is that your analysis of the market trend, the consideration of your trading equity at risk, and your current trading experiences must all lean in the direction of your market position. If you are long, make sure you are in a bull market, or at least that it is towards the tail end of a correction in a bull market. You can determine the current stage of market action by using various technical analysis tools. If you want to add to a profitable position, you must make sure you have enough equity in your trading account to cover the additional positions. This is extremely important because you must be able to add more positions without endangering the holding power of your total position. Rule 24 on pyramiding will help you understand what is involved in adding to your position.

Finally, your frame of mind must be good. If you have just experienced a string of losses and now find yourself in a profitable initial position, do you add on more positions? If you are disciplined enough to regard the previous losses as independent market actions that have no direct bearing on your current position, then you can go ahead. Most people, however, will carry their previous experience of losses into the current situation and will either overstay their position or overtrade their equity.

Second comes the psychology of profits and losses. Like everything else in life, your profit taking must be based on long-term plans. When you have a loser, your broker might tell you to hang in there, and you might think that your loser, given time, will come back. Or perhaps you think that you will offset your long-term losses against profits for a favorable tax treatment. It is exactly this treatment of losses that you must guard against. Losses must not be treated like profits. Instead, you must look at losses from a short-term perspective. If you lose money on a trade, you must get out of that trade immediately. Don't rationalize that these losses, given time, will be able to work themselves out over time. Profits, on the other hand, must be treated with a long-term view. If a trade works out to your favor, you must allow it to stay on the books and continue making money for you. Remember: losses must be treated with a short-term perspective and profits must be viewed as long-term situations.

David Garland, a fellow Treasury bond trader at the Chicago Board of Trade, made money by scalping the markets every day for a number of years. One day he was incensed about his day's trading. He sold the top of the bond move. He had unloaded 30 bonds right on the high of the move.

He said he sold the 50 lot at 89-12/32 and covered the 30 bonds at 89-10/32. He made two ticks on 30 contracts, which wasn't a bad day's trade. It was 60 ticks at $31.25, or something like $1,800. The bomb was that the bonds were now at 85-10/32, or four points lower. Each point represented $1,000, so on the 30 contracts he could have made $120,000 in three days. He sold the high tick but only made two ticks profit per contract. Three days later, it could have turned into a profit of $4,000 per contract.

I told him that he had no right to complain about his lost profit potential. After all, as a scalper he makes trades every day, looking to make only a few ticks here and there. If he does enough volume he will make a very good living by scalping ticks. When he sold the top tick, he was a scalper. When he covered his shorts two tick slower, he was still a scalper. But when he complained about the four points he could have made on the 30 lots, he was thinking like a position trader. As a position trader, he would have been able to carry the position to three days and make the full four points on each contract, but he would have had to come up with the margin money to handle the three days' maintenance. As a position trader, he would not have had the chance to short on the high tick. Position traders do not think like this. Scalpers do.

As a scalper David scalped into the high tick, but he wanted to ride the position as a position trader. This requires tremendous discipline. I have yet to find a trader who can do both well. You are either a scalper or a position trader. You are either a position trader or a day trader. You cannot be both in the same role.

As an outside trader, you can do this by opening two separate accounts and treating one as a trading account and the other as an investment account. You can trade IBM in one account and position IBM in another account, each with its own approach. If IBM seems like a bad day trade, close it out of the trading account, but if it looks like a good long-term hold, stick it in the long-term account and forget about the minor fluctuations that a day trader would worry about.

Once you condition yourself to think along these lines with the separate accounts, you will find it easier to cut your losses when you are wrong and let your profits run when you are right.

RULE 18

LIQUID STOCKS CAN BE COVERED MORE EXPEDITIOUSLY THAN SMALL CAPS

The chances for covering when trading short are better in a liquid stock with a large number of shares outstanding such as US, Steel, IBM, or Intel. Others with a small issue of shares may be more volatile and may jump a point or two between sales, thus hurting your chances to profit from trading short. So, do not short stocks with limited shares.

George Seamons, a noted writer of market books from the 1930s, observed there were different types of behavior attributable to different types of stocks in different types of markets. For example, the previous chapter showed that buying cheap small cap stocks at the tail-end of a bull market will show enormously high rates of profits. The converse, shorting cheap and small cap stocks, however, is not true; it will not necessarily give quick profits, but instead can leave the short holder vulnerable for counterposition rallies.

Let's analyze why. Keep in mind that in general markets which go up are not exact mirror images, both in form or function, of markets which go down.

One of my observations from professionally trading the markets for more than 20 years is that stocks and commodities must be "professionally" sponsored to go up. If they are neglected, they will go down without much effort.

If you are looking for a stock to short, you want all the odds on your side, all the factors skewed for your benefit.

For example, when you pick a stock to short, you don't want a stock that will shoot up against you. Lightly traded stocks, such as cheap and small cap stocks, shoot to the moon when the buying frenzy heats up. This automatically eliminates thinly traded stocks, which can violently move once the public grabs hold of them. What does this leave you with? Stocks that are moderately traded and those that are actively traded. Of the two, you skew the odds even more in your favor by picking a volume active stock because you're trying to find situations in

> *Shorting cheap and small cap stocks will not necessarily give quick profits, and can leave the short holder vulnerable to counterposition rallies.*

which not all the participants are fully aware of what is happening to their stocks most of the time.

The more players you have in this game, the greater your chances of getting the edge over one of them. Sheer numbers count even in this. Your objective is to move yourself into the category of winning traders and investors.

RULE 19

GO FOR THE LONG PULL AS AN OUTSIDE SPECULATOR

I started trading for my own account in the early 70s, when I bought a membership at the Chicago Open Board of Trade for $4,600. The Open Board was an exchange that traded the job lot contracts of the Chicago Board of Trade futures. Its claim to fame was that traders who started there and did well eventually went over to the Chicago Board of Trade. It was a testing ground for young talent.

Shortly after I became a member, the exchange changed its name to the MidAmerica Commodity Exchange. Several years ago the MidAmerica Commodity Exchange became associated with the Chicago Board of Trade. Now MidAm members trade in a separate room of the Chicago Board of Trade.

I learned a lot from the little exchange. I learned the value of patience. Patience, a very subtle investment approach, is something that we all know about but seldom practice.

The Open Board hired clerical help called "board markers," to record prices. They ranged in age from the very young to the very old. They checked for prices that flashed across the tape at the main exchanges and recorded them by hand on the blackboard.

I became friends with one of the board markers. His surname was Anderson, and everyone called him Andy. Andy was about 5'4". He seldom shaved, and he wore a battered trading jacket that peeled off his thin body. With his bad right leg he hobbled around the pits. He always hunched over as if he were looking for loose change on the floor. When I first met him he was in his late sixties.

He literally got paid nickels and dimes. At lunch time he would order lunch for the traders for a 50-cent fee. He had a pocketful of drinking straws and would sell one to you for three cents. After the markets closed, he would go over to the exchanges and pick up the free bulletins and trading data sheets. Then he would bring them over to the MidAm and sell them for a nickel apiece.

We became good friends, and I learned that Andy was a surprisingly wealthy man. Over the years he continued to add to his net worth. He never made any money in the commodities markets. He made his fortune in stocks. He took care of his older brother. His brother passed away several years ago and Andy, because of his lonely life, passed away by himself. He was a strange but lovable character.

In his youth he had been a clerk to old man Armour, the meatpacker. Andy saw how Armour caused his own demise. Armour figured that after World War II there would be more demand for red meats, so he went long the meats right after the war. His analysis was incorrect. Prices went down. Instead of liquidating his positions at a small loss, Armour bought more. At night Andy would go to Armour's safe-deposit vaults with the old man. There they would take out bushel loads of stock certificates that belonged to Armour's estate. Next morning Andy would deliver these certificates to the brokerage houses through which Armour sold his shares. Armour then used the cash to support his long meat positions. Armour went broke and Andy wound up working at the Open Board.

One day, after getting whipped in the bean market, I asked Andy for a good stock to buy. His eyes lit up as he told me about an interesting railroad issue play. Yes, Andy was a professional at railroad recapitalizations. Railroads, Andy reasoned, had many assets, and they go bankrupt all the time. He bought issues of railroads that went bankrupt and waited for the reorganization courts to distribute their assets.

This was the 1970s, and the country's largest railroad, Penn Central, had gone into receivership. It was just coming out of receivership. Andy was right on top of this play. He called me aside and said there was a Canadian railroad company that held a lot of old Penn Central stock. This stock was going to be called back by the reorganized Penn Central. In its place the new Penn Central would give new Penn Central stock, which the Canadian government would tax at an exorbitant rate. Before this could happen Andy expected the railroad to sell out the Penn Central stock. It would then distribute cash as an extraordinary dividend. The old stockholders didn't get much for their money. The new stockholders were able to buy the former assets at a fraction of the cost of the older issues.

> *Patience is the hardest part of trading and investing, but also the most important, for it is in the waiting that we make bigger profits.*

Andy expected the dividend to amount to $40 per share even though the price of the railroad was only at $38 per share. I looked at him in disbelief and said,"Come on, Andy. Isn't the market price going to adjust to reflect this?" He tried to convince me that the railroad, Canadian Southern Railway, had that exact play in mind, but I didn't think it would happen.

Andy looked at me as if I had given away a winning million dollar lottery ticket. He asked me to buy an odd lot if I had no interest in buying round lots. I thanked him politely and said that I didn't have the money available to take advantage of this particular play.

Four weeks later, the specialist suspended trading in the stock because the company announced a special dividend of about $40 per share. The stock went from $40 to $80 per share overnight. No one could find Andy the next several days.

I became ill thinking that I could have doubled my money in four weeks. I could have bought the stock on margin and tripled my investments. Here was good fortune staring me in the eye and I asked it for credentials!

As the week went by I found the lining to my stomach and put the antacid tablets away. I went to Andy and told him that he was right. He asked if I had bought any stock. Grimacing in pain, I told him that I had not. He bought early and heavily, hinting that he made over $200,000 on the play.

This is not the moral nor the end of this story. It is only the setup to the following sequel. Several months later I asked Andy if he had another play that could make so much money so fast. He paused to think it over and then said that he had tracked another stock that would be a very big money-maker.

My mouth salivating, my stomach acid churning, my heart palpitating, I waited for Andy to give me the details. He said, "It looks like the old Peoria & Eastern Railway will get a good settlement on the Penn Central bankruptcy. Yep, you gotta buy Peoria & Eastern. " I listened intently as he explained the details of the play. The Penn Central railway had rented feeder tracks that belonged to the Peoria & Eastern Railway. Penn Central wasn't paying the lease fees for the feeder tracks because of the bankruptcy. The move out of bankruptcy meant that Penn Central would make all the accrued lease payments to the Peoria & Eastern Railway. Stockholders and bondholders would benefit. It looked like another winner.

To garner more confidence in the play I asked Andy how much he was going to buy. He was so confident that he planned to buy not only the stock, but also the bonds. Penn Central had made no payments to its bondholders since the bankruptcy. With such enthusiasm emanating from his face, I just had to buy the stock.

I took money out of my trading account and bought several hundred shares. I bought at around $19 per share . . . all the way down to $14 per share. I was very bullish on this play. I even convinced a building contractor who was doing some work at our family business to buy 2,000 shares for his own account. Of course, I couldn't have convinced the contractor if I hadn't told him about the double-your-money-in-one-month play. We both looked at the play as another Canadian Southern Railway dividend play.

I bought and I waited . . . and waited . . . and waited. One month went by . . . two months . . . three months. I went over to Andy's corner after the market closed one day to discuss the Peoria & Eastern Railway stock play. Yes, Andy was still long. He was still buying. He asked if I had bought any for my account this time, and I proudly announced that I was long several hundred shares.

Meanwhile, I found lucrative trading opportunities at the Chicago Board of Trade. I moved away from the MidAmerica Commodity Exchange and lost touch with Andy. I would see him on LaSalle Street once in a while and I would ask if he knew anything about Peoria & Eastern Railway. Yes, he was still long and he was still buying.

Months turned into years. One year turned into two years, then another year. Three years had passed since I first bought the stock.

I watched the stock and tracked the bankruptcy court hearings. It was a thinly traded stock, so I had to read the pink sheets weekly. I even called up the only over-the-counter market maker in Peoria & Eastern stock to get price quotes. I showed up at all the Peoria & Eastern Railway annual meetings. My contractor friend, meanwhile, passed away. During one of the annual meetings I met his widow. We sat together on one side of the conference table along with another stockholder who wanted us to join him in a class action suit. Opposite us were the lawyers representing the Peoria & Eastern Railway company and Penn Central. I found it strange that the same lawyers were representing both railways. Year after year the lawyers told the stockholders the same thing: Rewards come to those who wait.

I checked the stock like an intern monitoring a patient on a life-support system. I had expected a quick one-month play, but this one would eventually span my trading career at three different exchanges. As I think about it now, I wonder why I didn't ever unload the stock. At one point it went down to $9 per share. Andy said he was long and was still buying. Would I doubt him a second time?

Three years turned into four, then five, then six, then seven. By this time I had forgotten about the company and the stock. Penn Central suddenly announced that all parties had agreed on a final settlement. For each share of Peoria & Eastern stock, Penn Central gave the stockholders $27 in cash and about a one-third share of new Penn Central stock. Penn Central stock eventually went up to around $70 a share.

I went to the bank vault to take out my Peoria & Eastern Railway certificates. I had them broken into units of a few shares each when I took delivery seven years earlier. As I look back at the reasoning I remembered how wildly bullish I was on this play. I expected to be able to sell these odd lot certificates in bits and pieces for huge amounts of money.

This reasoning wasn't to be. The markets did not repeat the first dividend play that doubled the price of Canadian Southern Railway in one month. The second play lasted seven years, but the money invested, around $15 per share, went to over $75 per share. The knowledge I gained by analyzing the stock over seven years and by dealing with lawyers and company presidents was very helpful to me as a stock market investor. I learned over the seven years of tracking the stock that it took time to make money in the markets. A get-rich-overnight stock had captured my interest and lured me into a long-term position because the fundamentals looked very good. This experience taught me the difference between trading for a living and investing for a profit. The difference is patience.

At the time I was learning this lesson, I traded in and out of stocks frequently. I got in one day and got out the next day. I bought Columbia Pictures at $2.25 per share and sold it for up to $7 per share. (Coca Cola bought a big piece of it years later at about $70 per share.) I bought Allied Products at $6 and sold it at $7. (It eventually got up to $34 per share.) As Peoria & Eastern forced me to hang on, my own trading strategy got me to trade in and out all the time. While my investment account was generating a 30 percent annual return, I was looking to make a few points in my trading account.

Patience is indeed the hardest part of trading and investing, but also the most important. We can study books and attend conferences on how to become better traders and investors, but it is in the waiting that we make bigger profits. This lesson taught me to buy Ralston Purina 0at 10½. I still own it. It traded as high as 92. I bought Tandy at 24. Now for every share I bought, I have four shares trading at 42.

No one can teach you patience in the markets. You are your own teacher in this regard.

RULE 20

SELL SHORT AS OFTEN AS YOU GO LONG

This rule was formulated years ago, but it is somewhat inac-
curate. It should state: "Be willing to go short as well as
long, but not as often." This modification implies that markets
go up as well as down, so if you are to be a professional trader
you must be amenable to shorting the markets also.

The original rule suggested that you should go short as often
as you go long. That is, if you are long for five trades, then you
should also be short for five trades. This is not the case because
markets do not spend an equal amount of time being bullish as
being bearish. In fact, it takes the markets more time to go up
than to go down. Given the same amount of price movement on
the upside as on the downside, the markets will take about
three times as long to accomplish an up move as a down move.

There are several strategies for accumulating a position,
based on the types of markets you are trading.

The first case is that of a grinding, up market. This is classified as a bull market. Since it goes up very slowly and
methodically, you can buy a portion of your commitment at
selected spots and accumulate more stocks or futures as prices
continue to improve.

When you liquidate positions towards the top of the bull
move, you should sell out your total commitment. Unless the
futures or stock has a wide sponsorship with very good depth,
the distribution at the top will often be shortlived, so get out
and take your profits quickly. If the stock or futures has wide

commitment and support, then you can take your positions off in a series of trades.

At the top of the market, the strategy for initiating short positions is defined by the way the market behaves at high price levels. Since price does not stay high for long, you should short your total commitment in one block. Once the move to the downside occurs, you will not have the opportunity to short more stocks or futures. If you are not already positioned for a downward move, you will have to chase prices down if you want to initiate short positions. Unlike an upwardly grinding market where you have ample opportunity to buy at your pricing, the crashing downside market will not provide you with opportunities to accumulate short positions.

Scalpers in the pits are attuned to the types of markets they are trading in. In grinding intermediate trends to the upside, intermediate and long-term traders can pick up contracts here and there. These slowly grinding up markets push the patience of the scalpers to its limits. The scalpers thrive on quick market action, and when they buy something at a low price, they want to sell it immediately. In bull markets, the scalpers, who are trading with much smaller amounts of capital, make money with great agony. Eventually, the prices will move up, but they have to hold on to their positions for three times longer than they are used to. When they are holding on to a position for a longer time period, they are exposing themselves to greater market fluctuation risks.

In downward markets, on the other hand, scalpers make a lot of money very fast. They sell short towards the top and, in about one-third the time it takes them to nurse a profitable upside position, they make the same amount of profits per trade in downward move.

The amount of money that was lost in the one-day crash on October 19, 1987 far surpassed the miniscule amount of money that was made by the scalpers on the downside. Outside traders, who were not trading with a short-term scalper's mentality, but from longer perspectives, lost hundreds of millions of dollars, while certain scalpers were known to have made $5 million.

I personally like to short bear markets more than I like to go long in bull markets, and I like to do so with a longer time frame. This is not because I have a scalper's mentality. I look beyond what is currently happening with my shorts and see market opportunities after I have unwound my bull market positions and before I institute my bear market positions.

> *As a general rule, selling short as often as you go long is not effective because the markets don't stay at the top as long as they stay at the bottom. However, you should be willing to sell as well as buy.*

Envision this scenario: The stock market is at the bottom of a long bear market that has spanned several years. I buy certain blue-chip stocks. Then the market goes up and prices become inflated. I add to my positions. After a while, I want to take my profits, independent of what I think the market will do. I unload my stocks and with my profits I look around to buy secondary issues that have not appreciated as much as the blue chips. I know that I can accumulate these at relatively bargain price levels. I ride these stocks to the top of their moves and then shift to the tertiary stocks. After I unload the tertiary stocks, practically everything is still high priced and inflated. I now find that the universe of bargain stocks has diminished. If I moved away from stocks, I could park my money in money market funds or other instruments that will pay me to hold their investments.

The following scenario of selling in bear markets is more to my liking: I have no positions and I see the markets topping out. The stock prices are overvalued, and one by one each leading issue rotates from distribution into weakness. I short a few stocks here and there. Individual issues start to crack and, in their first sell-offs, they drop dramatically. After the initial collapse, they come back to test their previous highs; then they start the slow, agonizing move downwards. I continue to short on the way down. When I am at the bottom of the price move, I cover all my shorts. With my profits securely stashed away, I look to go long on some real bargains. Not the relative bargains that I had to look for when I was at the top of the bull move, but

real undervalued assets of major companies. There are real bargains at this stage of the market's move. Stocks that were selling
at $60 at the top can now be bought for $6 per share.

My buying power for stocks is ten times greater at the bottom
than at the top. This is the secret to successfully playing the
short side. Not because I can make money fast, but because I
can buy real bargains at the bear market's bottom with the
money I made from the short side. For the sum of $25,000, I
could have bought a controlling interest in the whole RCA company at the bottom of the stock market in 1932. At the top of the
market in 1929, $25,000 would have bought an odd lot. Who
knows what opportunities await the bear market buyers at the
end of our current bull market?

As a general rule, selling short as often as going long is not
effective because the markets don't stay at the top as long as
they stay at the bottom. However, you should be willing to sell
as well as buy.

RULE 21

BEWARE OF SHORTING WORTHLESS STOCKS: DO NOT FORGET THAT DUST AND STRAW AND FEATHERS, THINGS WITH NEITHER WEIGHT NOR VALUE IN THEM, RISE SOONEST AND MOST EASILY!

Most people who don't have an idea of shorting often pick the cheapest stock to short. This is the worse thing that can happen. *Shorting* either stocks or futures is the process of selling these assets before owning them with the intent of buying them back at a lower price in the future and selling them later for a profit. This is the opposite of first buying assets for eventual sale. The ideal stock to pick to short would be the one that is overextended on a runup, regardless of pricing.

Let's address why this is the case.

One of the basic arguments propounded by people against shorting stocks or commodities is that the price of the short can only go to zero, i.e., a finite profit. The price of any stock or commodity, however, can go to an unlimited price on the upside, i.e., a long position can benefit from an appreciation that is potentially infinite. Given these two possibilities, why do professionals still short the markets, especially higher priced stocks or commodities?

The professionals only short two types of stocks: stocks which are on the highs of their extended runups, or absolutely (here again is the issue of subjectivity: what does "absolutely" mean?) bankrupt stocks which have no chance of becoming profitable. There are many more that fall into the first category than the latter.

> *A short position must be profitable much more quickly than a long position; otherwise the professionals immediately close out the positions.*

The time period to hold the short positions is also considerably less than holding outright long positions. If you took a look at the times that an open short position lasted versus one for long positions you will find that it is at the ratio of less than one to five.

A short position must be profitable much more quickly than a long position; otherwise, the professionals immediately close out the positions. At low prices, the chances of the price coming down dramatically is slim to none. There is some sort of value established by the public on the worthless stocks of at least a dollar or two. It will take a long time for $2 stocks to drift to less than 25¢ in value, even if the company is bankrupt. To go from $2 to 25¢ the short would have made $1.75, but the price had to drop 87.5 percent.

At high prices the situation is different for shorts. A 100-dollar stock price could dip to $95 in a blink and still only be considered to have lost 5 percent of its value. In a similar situation where the price drops to $98.25 to make $1.75 on the short, the percentage decrease is only 1.75 percent.

The chances of a stock fluctuating 1.75 percent, regardless of pricing, rather than 87.5 percent is much greater. The probability of profitably trading shorts rests with shorting the higher priced of the two if the absolute dollar moves are the same for both high-priced and low-priced stocks.

In the first example, there has to be a fundamental change in the stock's condition to justify a $1.75 drop. In the second, high-priced stock issue, a 1.75 percent fluctuation is par for the course in its daily trading—a mere technical condition.

RULE 22

DON'T BUY SOMETHING
BECAUSE IT IS LOW-PRICED

This rule, like most of the others, is valid when applied to the right market situation. The question is, how or when do you know you shouldn't buy at low prices, or sell at high prices?

There have been many cases where a stock price went to all-time lows and then went lower. There have also been as many cases where the price went down and then abruptly reversed to start a major bull move. What is low and what is high?

As much as I would like to say that I have some rules of thumb for determining "low" and "high," there is really no way to conclude from price activity alone that prices are low or high enough to accumulate or distribute stocks. To evaluate whether low is low, or high is high, you need to look at several aspects of market accumulation, price action, and time cycles.

In the cases of IBM, illustrated in Figure 22.1, and Elcor as shown in Figure 22.2 there were intensive accumulations as shown by On-Balance-Volume analyses at the low end of the price range.

In the case of Allied, Figure 22.3, the distribution pattern at the high prices showed topping action, but is still went higher!

It is foolish to assume that price activity alone is the sole indicator of whether or not a particular market is low enough or high enough to warrant investment or speculation. On the contrary, it is important to look at other indicators to help you make a more refined interpretation of market action. You can make your decisions to buy or sell based on volume and time-cycle activity, or a combination of all three indicators.

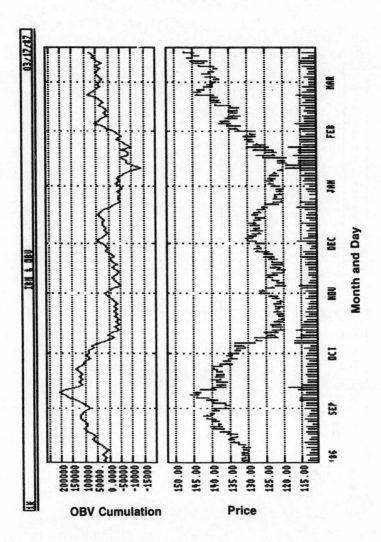

Fig. 22.1 Daily chart of IBM stock and on-balance-volume indicator, August 1986 through March 1987.

Courtesy of Equis International's Metastock professional software

89

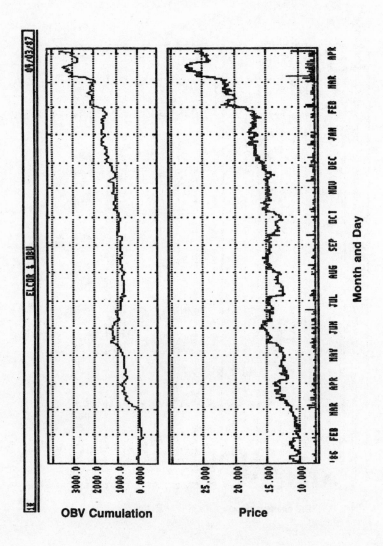

Fig. 22.2   Daily chart of Elcor and on-balance-volume indicator, January 1986 through April 1987.

Courtesy of Equis International's Metastock professional software

Unfortunately, the market is evaluated on price activity alone: the net price change from a previous period. You won't ever hear your margin clerk say that you will have to get out of your positions because record volume of stocks traded this morning. In the same manner, the clerk is not likely to want you out of a position because today is the second year's anniversary of the previous high. These indicators, however, are critical in helping you determine what low is and what high is, yet nobody in the business uses these indicators to the degree that they use price indicators.

The following points should help you assess lows and highs.

- Look at long-term price charts to obtain a perspective of where price has been in the past. Is the current price at historical lows or highs? If so, the chances are very good that the current lows or highs should hold.

- Try to put the correct phase of current action into perspective. Where is the market in relation to price-sensitive indicators like long-term and short-term moving averages? If the markets are bullish, old highs probably won't hold. If the markets are bearish, old lows probably won't hold. Use Elliott Wave analysis to determine the stage of market action, and weekly or monthly charts to see where price has been. Learn how the various technical indicators are behaving in the current market phase.

- Try to project price activity. You do not have to be right in your projections. By working over several possible scenarios, you set up your mind to accept what the markets will do. Look for the exception to the rules also. When you do this, you are less likely to be surprised when the markets do not behave as you expected. If future market action proves your analysis to be correct, then you are closer to correct market analysis and forecasting.

- Watch market action as defined by price, time, and volume. You must work on the assumption that when the market does go up or down that is what it will do in the future. This is not absolute, but it is the best that you can do. Don't fight the markets. Your role, as speculator, is to observe the market and make informed decisions based on your analysis of market activity.

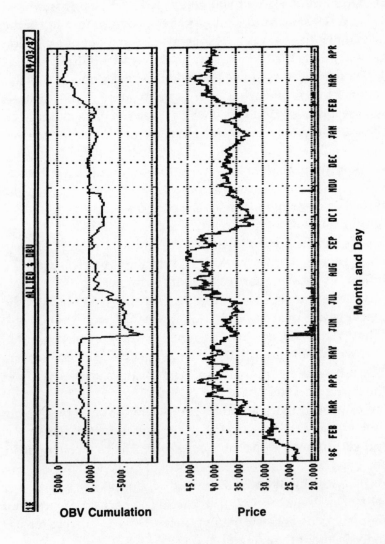

OBV Cumulation   Price

Fig. 22.3 **Daily chart of Allied and on-balance-volume indicator, January 1986 through April 1987. Note that price drops a little in May and June, then hits a new high, then hits a new low.**

Courtesy of Equis International's Metastock professional software

- Either buy at the lows, if so confirmed, or sell at the highs, if so confirmed. Otherwise, do nothing because the odds of making good profits are more against you in selling short into new lows than they are in buying into new highs. How much more money can you make by shorting a stock at $2, a new low, than by buying a stock at $200, a new high?
- Use short-term charts to enter the markets based on the direction that you decide. Once you have decided that the markets are low or are high, look for changes in trends. Watch price and volume activity to confirm your results.
- Always have an out in case your analysis is incorrect. Even though you prepare a game plan to cover your positions in case you are wrong, you must have correctly positioned yourself in the market to prevent catastrophic losses from inflicting permanent damage to your trading plan. A trading career is not made on one big trade, but on a series of profitable trades.

An interesting approach to buying low-priced stocks was used by John Templeton, chief investment officer of Templeton, Galbraith & Hansberger and Templeton Investment Counsel. Shortly after World War II John Templeton took an inheritance of $10,000 and invested it in stocks listed on the New York Stock Exchange. In a short article written about the great investing acumen of Templeton in *Forbes* magazine, Templeton disclosed that when he left the army in the 1940s he bought $10,000 worth of stocks trading at $1 or less listed on the New York Stock Exchange. His rationale was that the economy would be booming after the war ended and most companies would benefit from the increased business activities. Four years later, he sold out all his holdings and made a $30,000 profit.

> *To evaluate whether low is low, or high is high, you need to look at several aspects of market accumulation, price action, and time cycles.*

Most of the stocks went down and even disappeared from listing on the New York Stock Exchange. The ones that did go down obviously sold below their previous lows. With these stocks, the lows didn't hold, yet Templeton saw beyond the lows made by these stocks. Through a mere probability approach he allowed the ones that made new highs off their lows to make substantial profits for him. When he was wrong, he lost only $1 per share. When he was right, he more than tripled his capital. These winners showed huge gains in his portfolio. The ones that did bounce off the lows rallied and made new highs.

He used common sense to create his initial investment success. How much farther down can a stock trading at $1 go? With "low" prices like these and a portfolio approach to diversify the risks, investment success was virtually guaranteed. He removed the necessity of precise timing, which is needed now in our current investment and speculative climate, by first analyzing the direction of the main trend, and then investing with that directional trend.

RULE 23

STOCKS NEED SPONSORS TO BOLSTER THEIR PRICES; STOCKS DO NOT GO UP BY THEMSELVES

No stock has ever gone up by itself. However, stocks have come down without any support.

Over the course of the years watching and monitoring stocks I've come to the conclusion that you can find ways to discover how one company is dealing with another company. This information is available through out the information distribution channels, but you have to know what and where to look for them. The following details of a company-sponsored investment campaign will show you what some of these telltale clues are.

Let me relate an intriguing story to you about my own experiences with Hughes Tool stock which I tracked and monitored over the course of several years. Spanning several years, this example illustrates the dealings that go on all the time in the marketing of stock. This chapter details the acquisition, marketing, and apparent distribution of a company stock by another company.

The company was privately held. Howard Hughes's father created it in 1909. On December 7, 1972, it went public with hardly any fanfare. On January 28, 1987, 15 years later, Baker International Corporation combined with Hughes Tool and the companies are now known as Baker Hughes International.

Among the many companies supporting the upward price move was a company called Borg Warner, which later bought back its own stock and became a privately held company.

Borg Warner, now privately held, spun off two Borg Warner divisions: Borg Warner Security and Borg Warner Automotive. Borg Warner Security Corporation meanwhile has seen earnings drop precipitously. Borg Warner Automotive was spun off from Borg Warner Corporation in 1993. In October 1994, it held a second stock offering that raised more than $66 million to fund company operations. Recently the price of these stocks has dropped tremendously. Draw your own conclusions. As a private company it no longer has to disclose its finances to the public.

> *I've come to the conclusion that you can find ways to discover how one company is dealing with another company.*

Before Borg Warner became a privately held company, I became interested in Hughes Tool stock. However, I didn't know about the link between the two companies until I was pretty heavily involved trading Hughes Tool stock for my market maker account at the Chicago Board Options Exchange about 15 years ago.

Beefing up Hughes Tool stock after positioning the stock

According to the Hughes Tool annual statement, Borg Warner sold one of its divisions, Byron-Jackson, to Hughes Tool in October 1974; Borg Warner received 500,000 shares of $6.25 cumulative convertible preferred stock in Hughes Tool. The conversion rate was 7.5 shares of common for each preferred.

The investment in the Hughes's stock was carried at net book value of the Byron-Jackson operations at the effective date of the transaction and is reflected in "noncurrent assets." (Annual Report, 1975, Borg Warner).

Several years later, Borg Warner sold Centrilift to Hughes Tool for additional stock, but this time it was straight common stock, not cumulative preferred. In Borg Warner's 1979 Annual Report, Chairman Bere of Borg Warner was asked why it sold Centrilift to Hughes Tool for stock. In the process of explaining this, he also disclosed why Borg Warner sold its Byron-Jackson operations to Hughes Tool:

A bit of background might help explain our reason. Borg Warner already owned 3.75 millions shares of Hughes's common stock in exchange for our oil well service operations in 1974. This has proved to be a very successful transaction for both companies. Because the sharply focused nature of Hughes Tool closely matched that of the unit we sold them, that unit has grown and prospered to a greater degree as part of Hughes than would probably have been the case had it remained part of Borg Warner. In exchange, our investment in the form of Hughes stock has proved a very satisfactory one for Borg Warner shareholders. We expect the same will be true of Centrilift. The additional 1.2 million shares of Hughes Tool common stock we would receive would give Borg Warner slightly more than 20 percent of Hughes Tool stock outstanding. This would permit us to include that share of Hughes' profits in our future earnings. Because of the future growth we expect for both Centrilift and Hughes, we believe the transaction will allow Borg Warner shareholders to participate more fully in the vital energy market.

(Borg Warner 1979 Annual Report)

This statement shows that Borg Warner was deliberately beefing up Hughes Tool's earning prospect. So the positioning stage of Hughes Tool stock started as early as 1974, possibly earlier than 1972 when the company became public. This stage was brilliantly executed: Borg Warner got paid to hold stock in Hughes Tool in the form of a cumulative preferred. With the cumulative preferred, Borg Warner was getting paid the going market interest rate to hold Hughes Tool stock. I've discovered when the insiders play in the marketplace, they make sure all costs are covered. And the preferred was convertible to stock.

Value is discovered and the price moves up

Bere had admitted that his company, Borg Warner, had positioned in Hughes Tool. Then he disclosed that the next acquisition by Hughes Tool of Borg Warner's Centrilift division would also be beneficial to Hughes Tool.

Hughes Tool paid Borg Warner 1,200,000 shares of Hughes's stock for Borg Warner's Centrilift. In the process of doing so, Borg Warner now owned close to over 20 percent of Hughes Tool. The accounting procedures kicked in: Borg Warner now could incorporate the earnings of their holdings in Hughes Tool into Borg Warner's earnings statement. Overnight, Borg Warner which had been holding Hughes Tool stock in the form of nonearning assets, now had assets which were earning as much as Hughes Tool stock showed . . . earnings from which Borg Warner's formerly owned division, Byron-Jackson, and now formerly owned Centrilift, contributed to Hughes Tool!

James Bere became Borg Warner's Chairman of the Board and Chief Executive Officer in 1972. In 1974, Bere became a director of Hughes Tool. A year later, in 1975, Raymond M. Holliday, the Chief Executive Officer of Hughes Tool since the company became public in 1972, became a director at Borg Warner! Cross directorships! Some interesting things were about to happen.

Telltale clues forecast a price move

I started to monitor the stock when I became a member of the Midwest Stock Exchange's Options market. At the time that I was tracking the unfolding of the eventual runup of Hughes Tool stock, I was applying the on-balance-volume (OBV) technique developed by Joseph Granville. I became a devoted subscriber to his service for several reasons: He developed the accumulation indicator and he was getting a lot of press at the time. It was strictly out of a defensive posture that I needed to know what his thoughts on the markets were.

I was also using another technique, the Elliott Wave theory developed by Ralph Elliott in the early 1930s and currently espoused by Robert Prechter.

The stock had been trading in a tight range for several years. Granville published listings of stocks that he was bullish on in his newsletter. One issue placed Hughes Tool as a recommended buy. However, since I was tracking stocks with OBV I applied it to Hughes Tool and it did not show up as a breakout to the upside. The price started to move above the trading range—a clear breakout after years of base building. Puzzled by the lack of a buy signal using the OBV technique, I sent a letter, as a subscriber to Granville's newsletter, asking him whether or not my analyses of Hughes Tool using his OBV technique was correct. I received no reply from him.

Since I was also using Elliott Wave theory, by analysis of the stock showed that the current breakout away from the high range of $40–$42 projected to a market top of about $96 a share for Hughes Tool. I sent an inquiry to Robert Prechter of the Elliott Wave Theory newsletter. He promptly replied that he thought that the stock was bullish.

Meanwhile, as a young and unseasoned analyst, I told everyone to load up on Hughes Tool. Some did and some didn't.

The stock started to charge up. As an experienced tape reader, I noticed the bid and offers of the New York Stock Exchange specialist on the stock. It was being marked up. There was support coming into the stock because the bid and ask would show up a majority of the time with more stock being bid for than stock offered. The downticks would occur on 100 shares. Occasionally, there would be downticks of 500 shares. The upticks occurred on 1,000 shares or more. The upticks sometimes occurred on 5,000 shares blocks also. This indicated accumulation.

I watched the stock being marked up. It went up to $45 a share, rested and then moved up to the high 40s. If you were to go back to find a chart of the stock you would not be able to discern that the stock traded at $40–$45 per share around this time period because the past has already been obliterated and rewritten, with the use of several stock splits. The stock splits rewrote the highs and lows.

An insider but a peripheral player: the stock specialist

Shortly after I started monitoring the stock I traveled to New York on business. I was clearing at Goldberg Securities at the time and I asked the clerks and floor personnel of the company whether or not they could show me the New York exchange floor when I got to New York. I wanted to speak to the specialist of Hughes Tool. As a naive observer I thought I would congratulate him on his ability to mark up the stock.

When I arrived at the exchange Goldberg assigned a runner to show me around the exchange. I asked the runner to show me the Hughes Tool's specialist post. The runner remarked that the specialist was one of the oldest ones there, and he didn't even know if the guy was still around. However, this did not prevent me from wanting to see where the stock was traded. I likened myself to a tourist visiting in a new city. I wanted to see the sights that were of interest to me.

As I rounded the corner of the specialist post, the runner pointed out the specialist to me. I saw a congenial old man, with gray skin and a bald head. He wore a withered suit coat and was fiddling around with the orders placed in the slots in front of him. This was before the days of electronic trading, so everything was still done manually.

The runner went up to the specialist and motioned for me to move closer. I was introduced as a trader from the Chicago Board Options exchange floor. We shook hands, and as I stood on the outside of the trading post watching the specialist, he engaged me in conversation.

I told him I thought he was brilliant in helping mark up the stock. He looked at me cautiously, saying nothing. Then I told him that I was a market maker in Hughes Tool stock at the Chicago Board Options Exchange. This served to make me a member of the "club," an insider, too, if you will.

We discussed the stock a bit more, what I saw as the breakout and how I thought he was doing a skillful job of moving the stock up by tightening the bids and sloppily making the offers.

What then happened was unusual. The specialist motioned me to come over to his side of the post. He asked if I wanted to see his book of orders to buy and sell Hughes Tool. Of course I wanted to see it! What person who is involved in the markets wouldn't? As I moved into the post I saw in his eye a glint of "I'm going to show you something but you keep it under your hat" tone.

Then he showed me his book, which had about five orders, two on the buy side and three on the sell side, all several points away from the last sale. I cocked my head in amazement and asked the specialist what had happened to all the other orders. When I was market-making at the Chicago Board Options Exchange, I had noticed large buy and sell orders. There were always bids and asks from the specialist. He said there weren't any other orders. I asked him why there were so few in the book when I saw hundreds of thousands of shares trade daily on the stock. The orders must be there. He wasn't showing them to me.

He replied, "No. These are all the orders I have in my book. But let me tell you this, Bill (for by now we were on a first name basis), this is what I do: when the public comes in with orders to buy I sell them stock; when the public comes in to sell I buy the stock from them. This is all I do." When he told me this I observed a twinkle in his eye. First a glint, now a twinkle. I was now convinced that he treated me as a comrade . . . a comrade in arms.

I couldn't understand what he was telling me until months later back in Chicago as I watched Hughes Tool pop up close to $98 a share. The public and institutions were buying the stock all the way up. The orders I saw in the specialist's book were legitimately there, but other orders held by other brokers were never placed in the book. I would guess a good 90 percent of all orders existent at any time are not entered into a specialist's book.

The specialist, however, knew exactly where those orders were and who was holding them. At any time that he needed stock he could call these brokers to execute the orders, the specialist being the buyer of the stock. So, even though I only saw a few orders there were many many orders that no one, except the specialist and the brokers holding the orders, knew existed.

Because of the specialist's privileged status he could match the orders because of his knowledge. It was how business was conducted at NYSE. The broker made his commissions when the specialists called the broker over to take the broker out of his orders.

In the meantime, I saw the specialist put up bids and offers which gave me the impression as an outside floor trader that lots and lots of orders were bought and sold.

Although there were lots of orders to buy and sell, all were in the specialist's head, which could easily be "forgotten" or "remembered." This was all for the benefit of the specialist because the specialist could work his own markets closer or further away from the public orders.

There is no ethical issue here. It's neither right nor wrong for the specialist to be doing what he was doing. It's an accepted fact that that is how the game is played. Everybody in this business must follow the unwritten rules of profit making. It's as simple as that.

Stock price moves up

Meanwhile, the stock charged to new highs every week. I was happy because I was playing the stock from the long side. As the Hughes Tool scenario unfolded I began to sense more and more that I was a minute cog in the well-oiled machinery of stock distribution. It was one of the most impressive stock price moves I had ever seen in my 20 years of market observations, but I have neither seen nor heard about anyone else writing or discussing this story. However, a trader can learn much from it. All the support personnel have since made their millions and left the game.

This was happening between the last half of 1979 and early 1980.

Two other players entered the fray. One major player was Borg Warner. A second, albeit minor, player was Baker International.

I noticed one day that Hughes Tool was buying a French oil drilling company. Hughes was on a roll and I needed more drilling capacity. Imbedded in the Hughes Tool 1979 Annual Report was this obscure note:

In October 1979, the Company (Hughes Tool) acquired 90 percent of the stock of a subsidiary of Creusot-Loire for about $13,000,000. Beginning in 1980, the Company will use the two manufacturing plants acquired to manufacture rock bits and tool joints in France.

(Note 2, page 33 of the Hughes Tool 1979 Annual Report)

I thought it strange that out of nowhere appeared this obscure French company. The annual report did not mention it anywhere else by name. Elsewhere in the report, the company was always referred to as "a French company."

The French company was owned by Borg Warner. This was the first time I noticed that Borg Warner was involved, so I did more research. Borg Warner sold the company to Hughes Tool, the very company Borg Warner had stock interests in! Thank goodness for the unseen, but free, hand of market forces.

What I discovered later threw me for a loop. Hughes Tool raised money for itself by selling stock to the public. Among the many issues outstanding it had common stock and preferred stock. I found that only one company owned the preferred stock, namely Borg Warner. And this was a direct result of Borg Warner selling its companies, either named as Centrilift or the "Byron-Jackson operations." Aha! The trail gets hotter.

Mind you, now, this was all information I got through publicly available channels. None of this information was secured. Yet, by tracking this one stock I found correlations and connections that the average investor would never have found! Unlike a lawyer in a court of law, all I needed as a tape reader to draw my conclusions was circumstantial evidence. This is how most of the world operates. The hunter follows the bear tracks in the snow to find where the bear is. I saw my own "tracks." And they were indeed very fresh ones.

I positively concluded that Borg Warner had more than a passing interest in Hughes Tool. As the only preferred stockholder, it could ask for concessions and privileges others couldn't ask for nor get.

The questions in my mind evolved into, "If this is a price move, then there has to be a distribution of stock somewhere in the upper 90s price projection I had in store for it. What has happened to get stock distributed at this level? A new stock offering? A merger with Hughes Tool stock as partial or complete payment? What could it possibly be?" I didn't know who was involved. I was dealing only with what information I had.

The finale with a coup de grâce

At this time, the debt market was heating up also. Market interest rates were going up. They were at very high levels. So, what did the people at Hughes Tool do? They offered debentures to raise cash.

I couldn't figure out why they offered to sell debentures and possibly lock themselves into long-term commitments to pay high interest rates. Why couldn't they wait till the debt market had settled down? Why do it now? The marketers, whoever they were, created and sold products when the public wanted them. They created a product which investors wanted: high interest bonds with a play on upward stock price movements! A two-pronged appeal to increase the number of investors and speculators. Stop for a moment to think about what was done. Instead of considering that they were giving up the shop, they literally gave away the shop. I was really puzzled by this. Where was the protection from losing control of their company?

In April 1980, Hughes Tool sold $100,000,000 worth of 8.5 percent Convertible Debentures, callable and convertible to 1,602,883 shares of common stock. This was their protection. The convertible debentures were callable at the company's discretion. Before the year was up the stock had traded above conversion and, you guessed it, the convertible debentures were called.

The last step made me sit up and take notice. The Hughes Tool people offered debentures at high interest rates—the buyers would be buying this offering like crazy. As a kicker they made the debentures convertible to Hughes Tool common stock. Now, the debenture owner could have a guaranteed rate of return and also take advantage of any possible capital gains on the underlying stock. What finesse! What smoothness!

But still this did not answer the question of how stock was going to be presented to the public. Price moves such as these are worth nothing and are ineffective if you aren't able to unload stock at higher prices.

(The Hunt brothers implemented a patently illegal and more drastic attempt. This is something that they did not do when they attempted to corner the silver and gold markets. They accumulated the metals by laying their groundwork for acquisition, but they never laid the groundwork for distributing the precious metals they bought until it was too late. Their distribution stage was too late for them. Marc Rich, the notorious oil and metal trader, however, was careful in creating an infrastructure to distribute all the metals and oil that he bought and marked up. In the recent copper corner he was totally vertically integrated: he bought the mines, he bought the marketing companies, and he bought the refineries. In doing so he unloaded copper all the way through the various distribution channels!)

Hughes Tool offered the convertible debentures to the public. But they placed a string on their brilliant offer: they made the convertible debentures callable by the company. That is, the company could call in the debentures at any time and pay the full maturity value for the debentures. This was an excellent strategy. If the debentures were sold and interest rates were expected to go up, then the original buyers of the debentures would be sitting with mark-to-market losses since the value of the bonds would have to go down to reflect the higher market interest rates. If the company then called the bonds in the company would be artificially forcing the price of the bonds back to maturity value. What a great bonus to the convertible debentures buyers; these buyers had a hybrid put in place.

What brilliance. What acumen. I really wanted to get in touch with some of these guys in management. I was absolutely awed and amazed.

The price of the stock continued to chug on up. It traded above the conversion ratio. At this point it made sense to convert the debentures into stock and sell the stock on the open market and make a profit. The debentures had appreciated in value and now traded above their maturity value. Not because of the interest rates, but because the underlying stock. For several months, I waited for more news on the conversions going on. Nothing came through the public information channels.

One day, Hughes Tool announced they were forcing the conversion. All debenture holders had to convert their bonds to stock unless, of course, the debenture holders sold the bonds in the open market or back to the company for maturity value.

In one fell swoop, the money owed by the company to the bond holders had now been reclassified as shareholder equity, which took away the credit rights that they had enjoyed as bondholders. In one fell swoop, the IOU of the company to the bondholders had been converted to equity interests which had no effective block voting power. In Hughes Tool's 1980 Annual Report, the note under Capital Stock read "The net proceeds from these transactions were credited to common stock and paid-in capital." As long as the stock stayed above the conversion ratio, former debentures holders now holding the stock would not want to sell because then they would have to realize capital gains. Another way to make sure the investors kept their money in the stock!

Hughes Tool then announced another stock split. The company had split before. In the process of splitting and offering additional treasury stock, Hughes Tool had made sure the increasing stock position that Borg Warner held in Hughes Tool would never be larger than 21 percent of total shares outstanding. While the 79 percent that was held by the public got increasingly larger in numbers of shares, the depreciating holdings of Hughes Tool by Borg Warner was more than offset by the money Borg Warner made on buying and selling produces and services to Hughes Tool.

Drawing conclusions on a stock cycle

This was the end of the price move for Hughes Tool. Over the years I've watched the stock fall to the low teens. In April 1987, Hughes Tool merged with Baker International, to form Baker Hughes Inc. In the mid-1980s, Borg Warner acquired all the assets of Baker Industries, not to be confused with Baker International. But by this time I had learned enough of what power and force a concerted effort by moneyed interests can effectively do in the markets by using the right tools developed for the stock market to make similar plays. Other companies and other stocks have gone through this with even more planning and finesse. Sponsorship exists even today just as it did around the turn of the century, when the bulk of sponsorship rested with the market movers. The process of accumulation and distribution will always be with us. In this example, I saw and related to the reader the symbolic relationship between two companies: one willing to invest its cash and assets and another company which welcomed the investments. These will be kept secret till the day I pass on to the big exchange in the sky.

RULE 24

PYRAMID CORRECTLY,
IF AT ALL

In order to trade profitably, you must take a position in the market so that you can make money if the price moves in your favor. But even if you are correct in your analysis of price movements you won't be able to parlay your profits into more profits unless you have a plan to increase your position. This is why traders pyramid: They need to increase the size of their commitments to make bigger profits. This is where Rule 17 comes into play.

Another way to make more profits is to increase the frequency of trading without increasing your positions. This strategy is contingent on two factors: cost of executions and price skids. The best place to implement this strategy is the exchange floor, where all orders from the public are centrally executed and price skids are minimal. Successful floor traders are those who can combine increased transaction size and increased trading frequency.

In order to add on to an initially profitable position so that you can take further advantage of a favorable price move you must have two prerequisites. The first is that the market you are positioning in must be moving at a slow enough pace that you can add more to your positions; the second is that the market must have a sustained, one-directional move.

In pyramiding, you are looking for opportunities to add more positions with minimal risk to your total equity. Most successful pyramids have been created during massively bullish markets.

Few speculators have been able to pyramid successfully during bear markets.

When you decide to pyramid in a market, you are looking for profits from initial positions to allow you to either margin or buy outright more positions as the move continues in your favor. In bull markets, the price moves to the upside are slower and more protracted both in time and price. In reactions in bull markets, prices drop suddenly but start to recover their losses just as quickly. Eventually prices reach new high levels. As the bull market unfolds, the speculator has the opportunity to buy more positions in the direction of the trend.

> *In pyramiding, you are looking for opportunities to add more positions with minimal risk to your total equity. Most successful pyramids have been created during massively bullish markets.*

Pyramiding is not possible in bear markets because of the very nature of such markets. Bear markets go down fast and stay down. Reactions in bear markets, i.e. counter-trend up moves, are quick and brief. These reactions are quick to the upside because nervous shorts are rapidly covering their positions. These bear market reactions are brief in price stability because trapped longs are rushing to break even by unloading their positions at the rapid price escalations.

In bear market pyramiding you are looking for weakly sustained price action that will allow you to go short at the prices you want. Bear markets do not provide price floors for the speculator to sell additional positions within a reasonable amount of time. In most cases, before more short positions can be created the prices would have dropped.

There are also certain market-specific biases that make pyramiding difficult. In the United States stock markets, the person who shorts must sell short only on either upticks or equal ticks from the previous price. The short seller cannot sell on downticks. This in itself limits the possibility of the short seller entering shorts in bear markets moves if there are no upticks to allow the short seller to go short.

Secondly, the pyramid you build must be able to take advantage of a strong one-directional move. If there is no such move, then you will wind up just adding to a cumulating position at various prices that are close to your average price. There will be no price move that will cause your total position to appreciate in value. If a strong one-directional move does occur so fast that you have a limited opportunity to add on to your pyramid, you still will not have substantial profits accrued from previous positions.

A separate problem here is the ability to forecast when one-directional moves have the highest profitability of occurring. This is a matter for fundamental and technical analysts and, in extreme cases, for astrologers and readers of tea leaves.

Mechanically adhering to pyramiding can make substantial profits if there are also sound rules to enter stop loss orders so that losses can be minimized. (See the stop loss orders, Rule 11 and Rule 42, to determine what price levels to use in placing stop orders.) The basic rule of pyramiding is never to allow any subsequent position that you add to the total position to get so large that if there is a retracement the total profits are wiped out when your stop loss order is executed.

When you decide to pyramid in your next campaign, you must decide whether you will add positions in equal or varying amounts. From my own experience, I know that adding more positions but at lessening numbers is the correct way to approach pyramiding. Pyramiding in equal amounts of contracts or shares can also produce surprisingly good profits, but this requires a bit more analysis.

There are basically three ways to pyramid your total positions: inverse, normal, and averaging to market. Averaging to market is not a strict pyramiding approach, but it is included here because all the approaches are conceptually the same: You add more positions to your total position so that you can take advantage of future price appreciation.

The inverted pyramid is the correct way to approach pyramiding. Your initial position must always be the largest position of all your total trades; as more positions are added, each successive addition must be smaller than the previous ones. The mechanics are as follows:

Purchase No.	At	Buy Shares	Cost	Average Price
1	$75	300	$22,500	$75.00
2	$80	150	$12,000	$6.67
3	$85	75	$6,375	$7.86
4	$90	35	$3,150	$8.62
5	$95	25	$2,375	$9.32
6	$100	15	$1,500	$79.83
TOTAL		600	47,900	

As you can see, the number of shares added diminishes with the increasing market price. The average price of the total commitment stays close to the $75 level. As the market price increases, there is an increasing chance that the market is vulnerable for a price correction. The price correction of the market, if it truly is a bull market, will not, probability-wise, retrace close enough to the starting price of the move.

The second approach, that of pyramiding in equal amounts of shares, can also result in good profits. However, there is an inherent weakness in this normal pyramid relevant to the inverted pyramid, as illustrated below.

Purchase No.	At	Buy Shares	Cost	Average Price
1	$75	100	$7,500	$75.00
2	$80	100	$8,000	$77.50
3	$85	100	$8,500	$80.00
4	$90	100	$9,000	$82.50
5	$95	100	$9,500	$85.00
6	$100	100	$10,000	$87.50
TOTAL		600	52,500	

The inverted pyramid resulted in a total position of 600 shares with an average price of $79.83. Total cost of the 600 shares was $47,900. In the normal pyramid a total position of 600 shares was also accumulated, but at an average price that was higher than in the inverted pyramid. The average price was $87.50 per share and the total price commitment was $52,500. The average price of the normal pyramid was $7.67 higher per share, and the cost for the same number of shares was $4,600 more.

The capital risk of the inverted pyramid is all borne out in the initial positioning. In the inverted pyramid, the risk on the first purchase was three times greater than the normal pyramid, a $22,500 purchase versus a $7,500 purchase. In the second purchase, the cumulative risk was $34,500 ($22,500 + $12,000) versus $15,500 ($7,500 + $8,000) for the normal pyramid, or about two to one capital at risk.

It is only after the second purchase that the additional risk capital increments are in favor of the inverted pyramid. In the third purchase, the trader adds $6,375 of stocks in the inverted pyramid and $8,500 in the normal pyramid. The risk of adding capital now swings to the normal pyramid: a factor of 1.33 times. In the fourth purchase, the trader adds $3,150 to the inverted pyramid and $9,000 to the normal pyramid: now a factor of 2.85.

What you see here is that when one begins an inverted pyramid, the risks to the market campaign are up front. In the normal pyramid, the risks are spread out over the cumulation pyramid. From a strictly mathematical point of view the risks are evenly spread out over the normal pyramid; however, market reality impinges on this analysis.

The market was hypothesized to have moved from an initial low price of $75 a share to a high of $100 a share, a price appreciation of $25. If the market were to reach a high of $100 a share and retrace, we could theoretically pose three possible retracement prices: one-third, one-half, and a full two-thirds retracement.

With a $25 one-directional move without a sustained reaction, we can assume with a high probability that a one-third retracement will cause the market to bottom out at $91.67 [$100 – ($25 × 0.33)]; a half-way retracement would cause a bottoming action at $87.50 [$100 – ($25 × 0.50)]; a two-thirds retracement would cause a bottom at around the $83.33 level [$100 – ($25 × 0.66)].

The average cumulated price for the inverted pyramid was $79.83 and for the normal pyramid was $87.50. The $79.83 price for the inverted pyramid is not within the two-thirds retracement price of the whole $25 move,whereas the $87.50 average price of the normal pyramid was reached on the second possible retracement scenario of one-half. With the average price of the normal pyramid, there is a two out of three chance that the retracement will force the trader out of his or her total positions at a slight profit (at $91.67 and at $87.50) and a one out of three chance with a break even or a slight loss (at or around the $87.50 level).

RULE 25

DECREASE YOUR TRADING AFTER A SERIES OF SUCCESSES

I went over to the Chicago Board of Trade in the spring of 1976 when the exchange offered prospective members a deal in which the exchange financed the purchase of three types of trading permits that could be converted eventually to FIM memberships (financial instruments markets). The FIMs themselves were eventually converted to AMs (associate memberships). The three different types of permits allowed holders to trade one of three new or developing markets: commercial paper, gold, of Treasury bond futures. I was one of one hundred people who bought permits to trade bond futures and one of three hundred who bought the permit.

Among the group that entered the trading pit in futures that year was a guy by the name of Chuck Cohen. Chuck was my age, so we immediately hit it off. For the first year, Chuck struggled to learn the ropes of scalping in the pit. He traded in small lots and as the bond futures markets grew in volume, he slowly found himself being edged out of the trades. He was wired all the time and would respond to each trade like a jack rabbit darting out of the closing teeth of an animal trap. At the close of each trading day, his jacket would be wet with sweat. Yet, he usually wound up breaking even during the course of the day. Every so often he would make ten or 20 ticks a day for his profits—usually the result of several hundred trades. Chuck earned his money.

One day, Chuck and I sat down to compare notes. He had a great trading day and had made over 30 ticks in bonds, or about $650. He was very proud of himself, and I was very proud of him. It is very hard to make money in trading.

We all hoped Chuck would succeed as a scalper, despite the fact that other traders, including his friends and colleagues, were profiting from his mistakes. In fact, the mentality in the trading pit is similar to that of the water buffalo in the South African plains who are under attack by lions and tigers. When they know that they are about to be attacked, they gather together in a circle and face outward with their heads lowered and their horns directed at the attackers. The buffalo know that they must form in this manner for the safety and protection of themselves and the others. In a group they can thwart all enemies; alone they fall prey to the superior claws and teeth of the lions and tigers.

In a similar manner, all traders know that their own financial viability depends on the soundness of other traders. They know that when they trade with the other person in the pit, that person must be able to honor that trade. They also know that if they lose money, they will lose it to the other traders or brokers. Yet, they all must stand together in the pit against the outsiders. The individual trader doesn't want to lose, yet he or she wishes that the other traders would also win. They look up to those who succeed against the terrible odds for success—a strange environment to work under, indeed.

One day Chuck had made a considerable amount of money before the day was half over. I suggested that if he was running such a good streak, he should go back in to trade for the rest of the day. He said, "No way, Bill. I'm going home to take a nice long bath. I deserve it." He disappeared for the rest of the day.

Later in the year, I talked to Chuck when he was on a losing streak. He continued to trade, despite the fact that he was losing. He didn't want to be beat by the markets, yet he wound up losing even more.

Chuck did exactly the opposite of what a successful trader does. When he was winning, he whimsically stopped trading. When he lost money, he continued to trade instead of taking a break.

There are trends in one's life, just as there are trends in the markets. When you are young and in college, you can go out

115

drinking at night and be ready to attend classes the next morning. When you are old, you need to rest, and even a small amount of alcohol will cause you discomfort the next morning. Go with the trend at the time. If you are trading and you are a winner there is no reason why the trend must stop. The trend is for you to follow; most people think that if they stop trading with the trend, the trend will stop. Trade until you encounter losers, then stop. When you experience a string of losses, stop and come back again. Don't try to hammer the markets.

> *The simplest rule is that if you are having a string of winners, don't stop trading haphazardly.*

In the same manner that you must know when to stop trading and take a rest, you must also change your trading style at different stages of your life. When you are young and your reflexes are razor sharp, you can be a good scalper. You can turn around at the drop of a hat and hit the bids and take out the offers before anybody else. When you approach middle age, your joints start to hurt if you stand in the pits longer than half a day. You flex your knees often and yawn when the markets become quiet. At this stage, you progress to longer term trading. When you are old, you position trade. This diminishes the capital risk that you take on and hence your level of stress.

These observations on the life cycle of a trader are based on the "rule of three tens," which I learned from David Goldberg, the founding partner at Goldberg Brothers. This rule points up how long it takes to become successful in the futures trading business. It divides a trader's career into three ten-year blocks of time.

You spend the first ten years on the floor scalping and making a living. You make money one day and lose it the next. Over the course of ten years you learn to make more than you lose, you learn the ins and outs of the business, and you gain the ability to scalp for a living. During the second ten years you really start to make money. Hopefully, all the lessons you learned in the first ten years are producing a consistent and solid income for you. During the second decade you must make enough money for the third. During the third decade you use the money you have made in the second to make more money. At the end of the third decade you should be retired from trading and making money from your investments.

This rule presents an expected time frame to learn the business, to trade the markets, and to retire. If you try to modify the market's sequential ordering, you will encounter nothing but frustrations. You must do what the markets want to do.

In the case of the rule of three tens, you know what one can and must do at different stages in life. But when the markets are trending, how do you know if the markets are set to reverse or will continue onwards? The simplest rule is that if you are having a string of winners, don't stop trading haphazardly. Using the simplest definition of a trend reversal—when you have a string of losers—then you stop. If you stop trading because you have had a string of winners and think that the odds are that the string will end soon, you are trying to impose your will on the market. Let the market tell you when to stop, and that is at the slightest hint of a trend reversal.

RULE 26

WHATEVER IS HARD TO DO IN THE MARKET IS GENERALLY THE RIGHT THING; WHATEVER IS EASY IS USUALLY THE WRONG THING TO DO

As a trading strategy this rule doesn't mean a darn thing. As a valid observation of your interaction with the markets you'll find this to be true.

I happened upon this by accident one day while I was scalping in the pits. People always taught me that when bidding I should always bid under the last sale. When offering I should always offer over the last sale. This downtick or uptick is considered the "edge" in the scalping business. By securing the edge every time I made a trade, I had that extra tick as a comfort margin; I could take a tick loss on the next trade and come out even for two trades. In this manner scalpers have a decided advantage over others because they bid and offer at the market price which they make.

Well, I did exactly this and discovered that it was nearly impossible to bid for something under the last sale and get filled. The same with offering over the last sale. I seldom got filled because everybody else in the pit was trying to do the same. Those who were able to get filled worked a lot harder than me to get the trades. These scalpers were able to do this day in and day out. As a result of being able to get the edge, these scalpers make a very good living. As far as I was concerned, this was a lot of work.

Sometimes I did get filled on my bid or my offers. When I did get hit on the bid, the market dropped even more. The same happened when I got taken out on my offers. The market always ran higher. At times when my bids were hit and my offers were taken, the market was always running away from me.

This was always the case with me because I never fought for the trades and as a result I never really "won" any trades. All the trades that I "won," or to be more correct, those that filled at my prices were essentially given to me by other traders or brokers. In other words, I was essentially the trader left holding the bag all the time.

However, whenever I fought in the pits for the trades with the other traders, I wound up with trades that were eventually profitable, or at least trades which gave me a one-tick profit cushion for the next trade.

As a younger man I scalped like this in the pits and did well. As I got older this amounted to quite a bit of work. The knees gave way. Standing in the pits, fighting with the younger crowds, and scalping for ticks every day for hundreds of trades, turned into a chore.

When I never got hit on my bid or taken out on my offer I was really working the other side of the public orders. It was similar to the way I negotiated buying a car. When the seller agreed to my bid price I would then lower my price just a bit more so that no transaction actually occurred. When I eventually did make a low enough offer and the seller sold the car to me in frustration, I was assured that I had bought the car at the cheapest price, thus guaranteeing a profit! Buying a car in this manner was hard work, but I also knew it would never get me into trouble.

The same situation exists with trading the markets. If I continually lowered my bid when trying to buy I would buy at the lowest price and ensure that I would be able to sell it at a profit, or at least get the same price I bought it for.

But when I was more lax and did not want to continually

play this cat and mouse game I would get my bid filled rather quickly. In these times I knew that the positions I had acquired didn't have much chance of being profitable because the sellers would have more profit. This would further depress prices and I wouldn't have a chance to unload what I had accumulated. The easy thing always got me into trouble and it always had me long on a breakdown and short in a rally!

> *If you see a trading situation that requires investment of blood, sweat, and tears, push a little harder for you will have a better chance of success.*

The only way I managed to make money doing this was to continue doing it but also be aware of runners coming into the pits with orders in their hands. I would immediately jump into the fray and bid under and offer over, hoping that I would be one of the first in line to get the orders. This was really work!

As my trading progressed to longer-term position trading I noticed the same thing happening with research reports that I was trying to secure. I noticed the harder it was for me to get information on any stock or commodity the more often it looked like profitable situations. Following a stock like this for several years takes time and effort—it is hard to do.

The easier it was for me to get the research reports, the greater the chance that the rest of the world would have known about these profitable plays. As a result, the plays wound up being less profitable. This is why I really seldom subscribe to the investment letters written by the well-known market gurus. Everybody else knows about those plays. Give me some of those obscure writers whose analytical skills far surpass their marketing skills and I'll find a way to make money with that information.

Here's another example which might be closer to home. When working their leads for new business, excellent salespeople tell me they jump for joy when they get prospects who are difficult to reach for legitimate reasons such as doctors or lawyers who are busy all the time. These are the prospective clients you specifically want to go after, since no other salesperson has been able to reach them—the one persistent salesperson who does reach these prospects has a much higher chance of acquiring these prospects as accounts.

So, when you see a situation which looks like an easy lay-up, don't really pin your career on it—it may not be as profitable as you think, and may not last long enough for you to build a career. But if you see a trading situation that requires investment of blood, sweat, and tears—push a little harder for you will have a better chance of success.

RULE 27

Don't Formulate New Opinions During Market Hours

Successful trading requires many strong talents, and one of them is planning the trade. You must view the execution of a trade as part of a whole-brained approach, a gestalt.

When I was actively trading several years ago, I did most of my market analysis after the close. I would formulate a trading strategy for the next day and list the markets that I had to watch. When I placed my orders to enter the markets, I had a plan of entry and a plan of exit. If the markets behaved according to my scenario, I would hold the trade. If they behaved differently, I would sit back and observe their behavior. I had already established a strategy to get out of the markets if my analyses were wrong.

Most traders spend all their time figuring out what to do in the markets. They never give much thought as to what they would do if their analysis was wrong, much less what they would do with the trade if it was profitable. This is the main reason they lose money in the markets. If the markets don't behave according to their half-hatched trading strategy, they grab at anything—ideas from their brokers or what they read in the Wall Street Journal that morning. This information will serve as the crux of their new trading strategy.

In January 1989, the market traded in a range of 2,200 at the high end and 1,900 at the low end and had been in that trading

range for the last year. A friend of
mine had a strategy to sell at the high
end of the range and buy at the low
end. Premium sellers of calls and puts
were raking in the money. My friend
called me and told me that he had
bought a bearish put spread with the
Dow industrials at around the 2,175
level. He planned to leg off one side of
the put spread when the market
dropped. He actually had two positions on. He would liquidate one side
of one spread and hang on to the other

> *If you try to change
> your strategy
> during the trading
> day based on new
> market action or
> new information,
> you probably won't
> have the full
> resources to make
> an informed
> decision.*

spread position as a single position. If the market went up from
there, the amount of money that he paid for the spread would
be the most he would lose. His total risk was known up-front.

The market dropped about 100 points, and he saw his spread
widen in his favor. Up to this point, his strategy played out
exactly as he expected it. After the market bottomed out at
2,080, it started a move upwards and broke through previous
highs at around the 2,206 level. At this point, my friend had
planned to hold onto his position and watch the spread erode to
the maximum loss. That was the original game plan. Instead of
legging off one side of one spread when the price dropped, he
legged off one side of the spread at the new high level of the
Dow industrials. This was his first mistake.

He might try to rationalize his mistake by saying that his
strategy was incomplete, but I would disagree. He had a strategy if the market went down, and he had a strategy if the
market went up. He just never executed a part of his plan. Call
it a lack of discipline or whatever you wish, but he never followed through on what he originally intended.

My friend might also argue that he saw new data that the
needed to input into his original strategy. I would say that if he
designed the original strategy for a certain market scenario he
should not tinker with that strategy if the scenario no longer held.

My friend had originally allowed for a $1,500 loss on two
bear put spreads. Instead, he wound up with one $2,000 loss on

one spread that he liquidated and a $1,000 loss on the second spread that he held. An original loss of $1,500 was doubled to a $3,000 loss.

The lesson in this example is not to change your original strategy. Instead, carry out a new strategy with a new set of approaches. If you analyzed the market originally to be bearish and designed positions that would take advantage of a bear market, you must continue through with that analysis. If the market conditions become more bullish, you cannot tamper with the original strategy. You must liquidate the strategy as originally planned, then redesign and reimplement a new strategy geared to the new market conditions. If you try to change your strategy during the trading day based on new market action or new information, you probably won't have the full resources that you would normally have to help you make a more informed decision.

The correct approach is to analyze the markets first. Design a strategy or entry point where you want to position yourself in the markets. Plan where you will exit and where you will put trailing stop orders if your analysis is incorrect. Plan orders that will allow you to squeeze the market movement for maximum profits; then wait for the market to come to you.

I like to relate a story about Texas Slim, a professional gambler, because it shows how to approach the markets successfully. After one particularly grueling tournament that he won, a spectator in the audience went up to him and asked him to play a game of ping-pong for several hundred thousand dollars. Texas was a professional poker player, and he didn't know anything about table tennis, but the spectator finally talked him into playing the game with him. Texas obtained one concession: He would play with his own paddle. The spectator agreed, on the condition that he would play with the same paddle to equalize everything.

Texas practiced his ping-pong game day in and day out. When the day came for the match, he walked into the playing room, reached into his carrying bag, pulled out an empty pop bottle, and handed it to the spectator. Then he pulled out another empty bottle and told his opponent that he was ready to play. The empty bottles were the paddles!

Needless to say, the spectator lost, despite the fact that he was probably the best ping-pong player around. An unlikely paddle like pop bottles became the strongest tool that Texas could have used to win the game. He forced his opponent to play a game in which he did not know how to use the tools.

The markets are always forcing you, the unsuccessful speculator, to trade on their terms. What you must do is control your environment to the point that you take the risks that are on your side. There is no failure with adequate preparation. Those who fail in trading the markets fail because they don't know what to do with the tools that they have. The markets are erratic, and it is your role as a successful trader to isolate these random movements with your knowledge and experience so that you can predict market movements.

RULE 28

DEFINE MARKET ACTION FIRST, THEN TAKE APPROPRIATE ACTION

A trader friend complained to me about a trading system which he had developed, but he did not tell me whether it was a trading market system or a trending market system—because he didn't know. Both systems are valid under certain conditions. He made money with his system continuously.

One day the copper market started a massively bullish move to the upside. He complained that his system got him short on the way up and he had to continually cover his shorts. As a result, he was going to throw out his trading system.

This trader, however, was unaware that he was applying a trading system to a market condition which had changed. If you could personify a trading system, he should have thanked it, instead of shunting it aside. He was going to throw out all his tedious research and look for some other method to trade.

By now it was apparent to me that he was really using a trading market system: he sold the highs and bought the lows. So I suggested that he take a look at his system again. Had he created a trending market system he would have taken long positions in anticipation of the bullish move. The copper market had become congested for a number of months, which accounts for the profits he had made with his trading market system.

The copper market now trended instead of traded. How could my friend, the trader expect a system, a static system at that, to

> **All systems are static. They cannot adapt to new market conditions.**

adapt to a changed market condition? His actions and comments indicated that he had expected the system to modify itself for the newer conditions. Traders essentially take real-time data and constantly retrofit the data for constantly shifting parameters used in fixed formulas. Not only are you shooting at a moving target, you're also moving as you attempt to shoot the target!

As a matter of fact, all systems are static. They cannot adapt to new market conditions. Even the new strategies and techniques in vogue which have been recently developed around neural nets and artificial intelligence are static. Neural nets claim to take current market information and make forecasts with the most recent modified information; this is adaptive and not predictive. It's adaptive because it is still form and curve fitting brought closer, albeit, to real-time.

The trader agreed that he was actually using a trading market system! Before he continued on his path to discover the trending market system I suggested to him that, instead of throwing out the trading market system, he use the information given off by this system as a clue to other situations. The fact that he was losing money with a trading market system disclosed an important piece of information: those indications showed that he was no longer in a trading market!

Always look for the obvious and then read between the lines. The new information you garner can be as subtle as seeing the answers from a different perspective. By redefining the results of his trading market system in a new market condition which did not offer profits, he could easily confirm this was most likely a trending market.

He, therefore, had to change his approach. If he hadn't done this he would have forever been cursing the trading market system for having done him wrong, when in reality he was using a tool which couldn't be expected to perform under the new market conditions. Keep in mind that some approaches work in trading markets and some approaches are better suited for trending markets.

RULE 29

DON'T FOLLOW THE CROWD— IT'S USUALLY WRONG

This original rule has been around so long that most people today immediately dismiss it as contrarian trading and investment psychology. Let me be a bit naive and ask: What is the trading crowd? Where is the crowd headed that I don't want to follow? Is the crowd ever right?

And if you are a crowd follower, you won't be able to run out the door at the same time as everyone else when someone says "Fire" on the trading floor. The problem that we all have about following or not following crowds, running out the door or staying inside, is that we don't know what the crowd is, or what running out or staying in entails.

When you decide to buy something, you don't want anybody to find out about your investment. Only after you have taken a position do you want the crowd to follow you and buy the same investment. With their later buying, you can sell to them if you need to, and their buying makes your holdings more valuable. You can buy at the same time as the crowd, but you won't make as much as you would have had you bought earlier. However, you cannot sell when the crowd is selling. Getting ahead of the crowd is very critical when you are selling.

With the current milieu of government agencies beefing up regulations and grey area trading by exchange members, you must be sure that you aren't in the position of influencing investors. If you want to tout your long positions, you can't write about it in your newsletter or tell your employees in the bank's trust department to buy. This is strictly prohibited in the interest of fairness.

Crowds can be right at times and can even cause markets to fool the professionals. Every so often, the crowds can wrest control of the markets away from insiders and professionals and give these players a run for their money. This is where the term "oversold bull" originates. When the markets go higher after your analysis has led you to take your profits, the markets can continue straight up and cause the most astute insiders to unload their holdings at market's new highs. The problem doesn't end here for the professionals. Most of the damage occurs when the market continues even higher. The professionals, having already gotten rid of their long positions, now institute a short selling program. (It's so difficult to buy again after you have made a substantial amount of money on a major position.)

The quandary posed to the professional when the public takes hold of the market applies not only to bull markets, but also to downside markets. Horror stories abounded after the October 19, 1987 worldwide market crash. Friday, October 16 was the first day of the massive downdraft. Many professionals who were still in business on that day told me that they had substantial profits on Friday's close. They came into the markets Monday opening short and made embarrassingly huge amounts of money immediately at the opening bell. As one professional told me: "I couldn't help myself. The market just handed me fistfuls of money." It was what happened during the rest of that Monday, October 19, that did these professionals in. The market opened much lower, rallied, and then sold off dramatically. On the opening, some pros covered shorts. As the market went lower, they started to go long at 150 points lower, then 200 points lower, then 300 points lower, then 400 points lower. It looked as if the lows of the century were going to be tested. At the bottom they sold all their positions.

I wouldn't say that this day was under direct control of the public—How can you say that one has control of one's body when hurtling over a cliff screaming, "I'm sure I will hit bottom!" The effects were the same, nonetheless. The public went over the cliff at the same time, and the professionals tried to support the falling bodies. Who was smarter? Public speculators and investors in the back pushed the public in the front into the chasm, all the while getting a bigger and bigger crowd to follow.

> *Every so often, the crowds can wrest control of the markets away from insiders and professionals and give these players a run for their money. This is where the term "oversold bull" originates.*

When I first started to trade grains at the MidAmerica Commodity Exchange in 1972, I saw soybeans go from $4 a bushel to well over $12 in July deliveries. Wheat prices topped out around the $6 level and cornwent up to $4 a bushel. The highs of the soybean markets of 1972–1973 haven't been surpassed even as of this writing. In the process of doing this, the markets fooled the professionals, and many floor traders lost their shirts. Prior to this massive bull move, the highs in the beans were around $5 per bushel.

Around the first new highs, professionals went short by selling the front months and buying the back months—they created bear market spreads. As beans went higher, the spreads first went to even money. The price of the front-end beans contract was exactly the same price as a future delivery contract months later. There was a pressing demand for beans at the here and now. As the bull market continued, the difference between front-end beans and back-end beans became greater still.

The beans for delivery here and now traded well over the prices of beans for future deliveries. Because of the demand for the cash beans and the lack of available beans for delivery, the short sellers of outright positions and the biased short bear spread sellers found themselves caught in a squeeze. The bean shortage eventually reflected in the all-time high of $12.90 per bushel for July 1972 beans. The move from $6 to $12.90 meant a profit of $34,500 per contract of 5,000 bushels of beans. The bearish short seller did not see the spread move exactly that amount, but the July/November 1972 (old crop versus new crop) bean spread went from a 25-cent premium to $4.90 per bushel premium on the front month, or $23,250 per contract.

Public speculators profited at the expense of the professionals. The masses were able to cash out to big numbers in this move.

The gold (Figure 29.2) and silver (Figure 29.3) markets were wildly bullish in 1979 and culminated in a high of about $800 for gold and $50 for silver. During the up move, everybody who had been hoarding gold and silver for the past decade cashed out. In the meantime, the professionals on the floor were heavily short and sustained tremendous losses.

These examples of specific cases where the public was able to take control of the markets from the professionals are stellar. Such cases make the headlines but don't make money consistently. Unfortunately, such occurrences are rare. In the last 20 years, only a handful of such publicly controlled markets have existed. Meanwhile, had you played along with the professionals, you would have made a substantial amount of money. As an outside participant with limited risks, you are in the unique position of being able to capitalize on most of these stellar moves.

Generally, the public loses money in most markets. Don't allow a few cases where the public had made money to influence you to take sides against professionals all the time. In the long run, my money has always been on the side of the professionals.

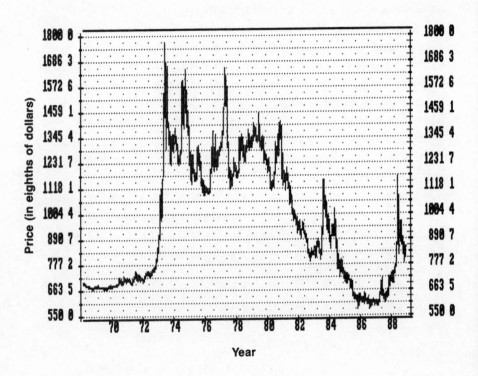

Fig. 29.1 Monthly continuation chart of soybean contract traded at Chicago Board of Trade, 1968–88.

Courtesy of Computrac software, version 2.8

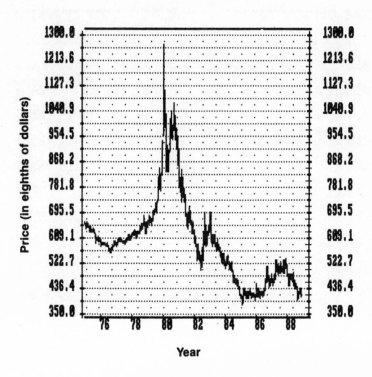

Fig. 29.2   Monthly continuation chart of gold contract traded at Commodity Exchange, 1975–88.

Courtesy of Computrac software, version 2.8

133

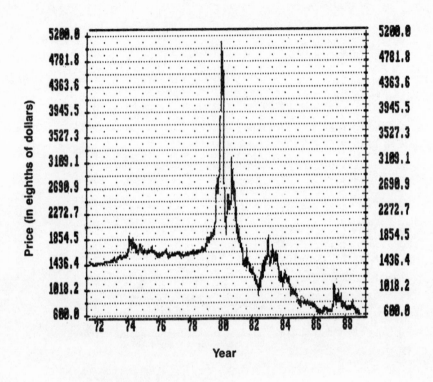

Fig. 29.3 Monthly continuation chart of gold contract traded at Commodity Exchange, 1975–88.

Courtesy of Computrac software, version 2.8

134

RULE 30

DON'T WATCH OR TRADE TOO MANY MARKETS AT ONCE

A remarkable salesman told me years ago that the human mind is a wonderful thing: It can process millions of thoughts at the same time. Unfortunately, because of the limits of the five senses, only one or two of these thoughts can be externalized at any point in time. He likened it to trying to fill an empty bottle by pouring water into it through a funnel. The water accumulates at the funnel's top, but it still has to drop slowly through the opening at the bottom. Try as you might, if you pour water into the funnel at a faster rate, the water will not go through any faster than the bottom of the funnel will allow.

The same can be said for trading many markets. The fact that there are more than 6,000 stocks, an infinite series of options on those stocks, more than 50 futures contracts and an infinite series of options on those futures, ever-expanding debt instruments, and so on, ad absurdum, offers you, the trader or investor, a myriad of speculative and investing opportunities.

When I started trading, I had lots of time but no capital. I thought then that capital placed an absolute limitation on trading opportunities. Now that I am in my forties, I have lots of capital, lots of opportunities, but no time.

The amount of capital that you can use to play in the markets does limit the number of issues you can track. If you have a lot of money, you can trade a lot of markets. If you have a small amount of capital, you have to become more of a money manager than a manager of positions. When the unseasoned trader

> *Fewer and fewer people know how to manage money well, while the number of people who have funds to be managed and are computer illiterate is increasing.*

looks at any market with a keen eye for margin leverage, the door is open for abuses of capital management. The question then is, What do you do with the capital you have, and how do you do it?

If you took the easy way out and placed all your capital into one investment, then you could watch it diligently. But is this the best way? Isn't there a more effective way of investing a fixed amount of investable or tradeable funds by increasing the number of markets or instruments that we invest in? The other approach is to go to the extreme and buy a few contracts here, a few of another there, until all the investable funds are thoroughly diluted among 20 or 30 investment or speculative vehicles.

Peter Lynch, the funds manager for the Fidelity Funds, is so spread out that he is invested in several thousand stocks. The mass of his investable capital is so large that he can't stay in the area of stocks and remain a successful money manager. Several years ago, a money manager for the Prudential Insurance company said that he could no longer invest in stocks because he had so much money. He said that if he were to shift to the stock area completely, he would be able to buy the capitalization of the New York Stock Exchange blue chips several times over and still have money left over.

Jack Gaumnitz, while he was working on his doctorate degree at Stanford University in 1967, studied the diversification of risk in a portfolio of securities. He discovered that once the number of securities in a portfolio reached 18, risk could no longer be lowered effectively through diversification. Another doctoral student at the University of Washington, John Evans, discovered in 1968 that five randomly selected securities in a portfolio proved to be as risky as 2,400 tested portfolios with one to sixty randomly selected issues. Evans diversified by investing equal dollar amounts in a given number of stocks; in other words, if he started with $50,000 as a portfolio, he would create portfolios of five randomly selected stocks with $10,000 invested in each, all the way to sixty randomly selected stocks with $833.33 invested in each. The conclusion reached by Chris Mader and Robert Hagin, authors of *The Dow Jones-Irwin Guide to Common Stocks*, 1976, was that "a typical portfolio with equal dollar amounts in just five stocks, selected for diverse risk characteristics, will have only slightly more risk than would be attained by placing equal dollar amounts in all stocks." Therefore, it isn't necessary to track all the markets, nor is it necessary to trade only one closely watched market in order to diversify your risk and limit exposure of capital.

Their experiences might not be directly applicable to you, but you do have the resources nowadays to track historical price action, forecast future price movements, and monitor news activity of a greatly increased number of stocks, futures, or options. With the advent of computer technology, what took several hours to do manually years ago can now be done instantaneously.

I tracked the markets that I traded and diligently charted their price and volume activity every day. When I went on the floor to trade, I narrowed the time interval from daily to hourly, then from hourly to every quarter hour, and finally from quarter hour to trade by trade. My tracking of market action by driving down the time interval got so ridiculous that at any one point I had more than 15 tick by tick charts in my trading jacket pocket. There were the tick by tick charts, the three-minute barcharts, the fifteen-minute bar charts, the hourly barcharts, the half-hour bar charts of the cash markets, the daily spread chart of the front-end contract versus the back-end, the daily charts of the major indices, the moving average charts, the oscillator charts, the relative strength charts with several different time durations, etc. Then there was the reports almanac I carried around in my vest pocket. It stuck out so I could easily look down to see what reports were being issued today, the next day, the next week, next month, even compare numbers from a year ago. The monster that I created got out of hand. The fun of trading got lost in the mounds of charts and reports I was tracking.

As traders are wont to do, I treated the problem of information overload by throwing money at it. I reasoned that if there was so much information available, so many ways to massage that information, so many markets to trade, so many derivative products from those markets, so many ways to do so many different things, it was certainly necessary to study these. I looked at the many tools available to study these many things.

The next thing I knew, I had computer overload. There were the Sphere, the Altair, the Imsai, the Apple, the Radio Shack, the Tandy, the Macintosh, the IBM PC, the clone, and the clone's clone. With these came the software packages to manage the miniaturized behemoths of computing power. The Dow Jones Stock Analyzer, Meta-Stock, Lotus, Window on Wall Street, Breakout and Out-break Systems, the Technician's Toolchest, Options Analyzer, Optionvue, SideView, and End to End. In effect, to be a minimal survivalist in this ever-changing market, I had to be a specialist in computer hardware, software, trading strategies, and money management.

Everybody can use technical analysis but most don't understand it yet. There is a void of understanding. The existence of computers has created a strange paradox of understanding. On the one hand, the computer software and hardware used in trading makes it much easier to trade: In a span of a few milliseconds, the trader can analyze one market. In a span of ten minutes, the world of investment analysis is at his feet. On the other hand, the average private investor doesn't know how to use these tools, which were once the province of heavy-duty money managers and sophisticated traders. Unless he or she has actually worked with these techniques, the average investor will be at a loss as to how to use them to trade the markets effectively.

Computerized trading technology has created a wealth of opportunities for money managers, but it also has bifurcated market participants: We now have people who manage funds and people who have funds to be managed. Fewer and fewer people know how to manage money well, while the number of people who have funds to be managed and are computer illiterate is increasing. As in the other areas touched by computers, the gulf between those who know and those who don't know is becoming wider.

As in all cases where technology over runs itself, computers can only benefit those who already know what they're doing.

The object of computers is to free up your time so that you can analyze a market with more precision, not to free you to analyze more markets. I think it is a good idea to go back and work some charts by hand once in a while to get the feel of the price action. There is something to be said for actually seeing patterns unfold when you add them to a chart. It's like going back to nature to get your bearings.

RULE 31

BUY THE RUMOR,
SELL THE FACT

Please note that the rule tells you to sell the fact, not buy the fact. Implicit in this rule is the assumption that the rumor is bullish. Rumors, however, can as easily be bearish.

Bullish rumors are what you base your buying on. Once the bullish fact is known, then it is too late to buy because the bullish news will have been factored into the market price. Instead, it should be sold. The idea, then, is to buy in anticipation of bullish news and sell when the news is out.

If the rumor your hear is bearish, leading to actual bearish news, then the statement: buy the rumor and sell the fact, does not hold. In fact, there is a greater danger to your trading equity if you buy on bearish rumors and sell on bearish news. Markets have a tendency to go down alot further and a lot faster than they go up. With this action, it would be foolish to establish a long position in anticipation of a bearish rumor becoming fact.

To establish a short position in anticipation of covering the short when a bearish rumor turns to fact is a better strategy, but not by much. The risk with this strategy is great. First of all, you don't know what the market has already discounted before the rumor becomes fact. This problem is inherent in all rumors. Secondly, there is a chance, slim though might it be, that the market you are interested in might even rally on the bearish rumor becoming fact. This would be attributable to the fact that the established shorts would use the bearish news as an opportunity to pull in their shorts.

If I have confused my readers with all of the above scenarios, I only want to illustrate the difficulty in trading based on rumors. I do absolutely nothing with rumors, and I watch very carefully when the facts come out.

How do you distinguish facts from rumors? The key is the source. Facts come from known and reliable sources such as government or corporate reports. The sources of rumors are unknown, so their validity is suspect. Rumors are created in the minds of traders who are trying to account for unknown causes of price and volume activities. If enough rumors are created around these observed price and volume activities, a few of the rumors will actually justify the heretofore unaccountable market action. When facts are offered, then the connection is made between these "valid" rumors and the facts.

> *I caution against entering positions in anticipation of government reports or other facts. The wise trader closes out all his positions and waits until the markets reopen with the news already factored into the price and volume action.*

The intelligent trader acts on the price action alone, with a keen eye on volume activity. If there is activity without facts, then something is going on, and it would be wise to close out positions by selling out longs or covering shorts. Only when the rumors actually become fact is it safe to re-enter the market.

For the same reason, I caution against entering positions in anticipation of government reports or other facts. Before any government reporting agencies make their announcements, the wise trader closes out all positions and waits until the markets reopen with the news already factored into the price and volume action. If the trend that existed prior to the announcement is resumed, then it becomes that much stronger. If the announcement is contrary to the previous market trend, the trader has an opportunity to watch a substantial test of the trend's underlying strength or weakness. Trends that are in force take time to reverse, so if someone is positioned in the direction of the main trend, and that trend is veritably killed by news announcements, that trader still has a very good chance to get out at a slight loss.

Initiating any positions prior to the news announcements is gambling. If you are wired to some government insiders and have access to information before the public obtains it, I urge you not to use that information in your trading. The immediate profits you make will certainly cause the governing agencies to look at your trading records. With the current regulatory environment on the nation's commodities and options exchanges, it would be foolish to jeopardize a lucrative profession for an inside trader's profits.

We all need hopes and dreams to give meaning to our lives, but wishful thinking can cause tremendous overstaying of positions. Wishful thinking comes about after a position has been instituted and the facts are already out, seldom before.

RULE 32

PRESERVE YOUR CAPITAL

In an environment outside of trading, the above statement has great impact. The amount of capital that you have determines how successfully you can extend your very existence from the present to the future. With capital, you can invest in properties and companies that have future growth implications. Without capital, you live for the present.

The same holds true for trading accounts and trading careers. If you have the accumulated capital you have control over your trading opportunities and your career development. Conversely, if you lack the trading capital then you cannot control your trading opportunities and career.

There are many ways to control the risk to which you expose your capital, but there is only one way to preserve capital: by thinking out your trading situation and determining where the risk to your capital lies.

Most traders are very intelligent. In fact, trading and speculation appeal to white-collar professionals with above average intelligence. Many retirees trade in the markets often. With their years of experience in life, they have more wisdom to draw upon than the younger traders. Yet, these very same people often wind up with no money in their trading accounts after a few trades. How does this happen?

Many of us suffer from what floor traders call the "King Kong Effect." We think that the next trade is the one Kahuna that will make the year. Instead, like King Kong, who fell to his death at the height of his glory, we often end up losing everything.

I lost a substantial portion of my trading account when I was learning how to trade bonds. I thought this play was a shoo-in.

> *Many of us suffer from what floor traders call the "King Kong effect." We think that the next trade is the one Kahuna that will make the year.*

The bonds opened lower that morning. My scenario called for a quick reversal to the upside. I had $10,000 in my trading account. The margin at the time was $1,500 per bond contract. Over the course of the years I learned the importance of controlling the exposure of my trading capital. As the market traded that morning, I initiated my first trade with two contracts.

I say "initiated" because I eventually bought more contracts. At the time of the trade, I never expected to add more.

As the morning wore on, the bonds failed to show any signs of strength. In fact, they moved lower, to below my first purchase price. I reasoned that I could not safely buy more than six bond futures because of the margin requirements—six contracts at a margin of $1,500 per contract required $9,000 to control. As the price dipped lower, I bought two more contracts. Now, I was long four contracts at an average price that was higher than the current market price.

I was not alarmed that the bonds didn't show any strength right then, but as the morning passed and the afternoon began, the bonds still failed to show any signs of strength. I again positioned an additional two contracts at new low prices. Now I was long six contracts in a market that looked like it might rally, once, to let me out of my total positions. The old bromide that markets do not go straight up or down, but trade in racheting up and down moves, came to my mind. I tantalized myself into believing that I was going to be given an opportunity to get out of all my positions at a slight profit.

Unknown to me at the time was the fact that my starting capital base of $10,000 was rapidly eroding. I acquired my total six contracts at lower and lower prices. The last lot was the one that had the price closest to the market price, i.e. that showed the smallest amount of loss or profit (in this case, loss) from the market price. The earliest position showed the greatest loss.

Because I was a day trader trading with a short time frame in mind, I wasn't aware of the erosion of my trading capital—the capital I use to maintain a position in the markets. What started out as $10,000 for two contracts was now $10,000 less the mark-to-market losses, and six contracts.

At $10,000 and two losing contracts, I had a lot of room to run around in. At $6,000, which was the current mark-to-market equity, I had three times my original position. Anyone could easily see that with my $6,000 I was trying to control six contracts. Margin, strangely enough, remained at $1,500 per contract. In the morning I had $10,000, two positions, and a wish. On the close, I had six contracts, $6,000, and an unanswered prayer. I sold all my positions on the close at big losses. I wound up with $4,000 in my trading account and no positions.

My trading equity eroded due to market losses resulting from increasing positions. I was getting nailed at both ends. First, my total position in bonds was getting more costly relative to current market value. Second, the equity that I needed to sustain these and other trading positions was diminishing rapidly. The market losses based on the increased positions hurt, but not as much as the trading ramifications from those losses. With diminished capital as a result of increased bad positions, I had to trade smaller contracts and work the remaining capital much harder to get my trading equity back to $10,000. This is why many people are more successful trading from a deficit account than with a positive equity account.

Now, as a seasoned trader, I look back and know exactly what I did wrong. Losses are a given in the trading business. However, uncontrolled losses due to bad position management can cause debilitating financial and career damage. The example of my trading bind shows that even a professional trader with a well-planned strategy can get caught up in the trading game.

In ending this chapter, my suggestion is that you first control all the risks to your trading equity; then worry about how high the Empire State Building is. See Rule 30 for more discussion of how to control these risks.

RULE 33

IF THERE ARE LARGE AMOUNTS OF CAPITAL, EMPLOY HEDGING

All market professionals have an aversion to market risks because these risks are, by definition, uncontrollable.

As professionals, traders have honed certain strategies or methodologies related to their special niche of moneymaking. For example, the scalper goes in and makes a trade by selling over the last sale and buying under the last sale. In this manner the scalper makes his tick, day in and day out. The arbitrageur will buy IBM stock traded in London and sell the stock traded in New York for a small price differential. The options market maker will neutralize his or her net delta positions by hedging the other side in the actual cash market.

Professionals are risk averse. Because they thrive in market risk environments they appear to be risk takers. They aren't.

On the contrary they will seek to "pass off" the risk to others as soon as possible. Note how many bookies in Las Vegas, who are professionals, will ever take on a bet without finding a way to pass off the risk to someone else? Note also, in the corporate world, how insurance companies through the use of the information derived from actuarial tables, seek to limit their risks? If need be they will pass off risks to re-insurance companies if they can't pass off their risks in their normal channel of operations.

The same applies to huge stock traders. Market risks are those unknown, unseen forces which cause the market to drop

> *Professionals develop methods and strategies to insulate themselves from these market risks. One strategy is to be perfectly long and short at all times.*

precipitously or rally like a rocket. Assassinations of political leaders, interest rate hikes, earthquakes, and other natural disasters are some of the factors which translate into market risks for professionals.

Professionals develop methods and strategies to insulate themselves from these market risks. One strategy is to be perfectly long and short at all times in the stock market. Let's take a look at how this is done and how best to execute this strategy.

If you have $1,000 to trade the markets you really only buy stock. You couldn't short stock without opening a margin account. You might buy 300 shares of Tucson Electric Power, now trading at $3.50 a share. This is all you can do. If the company goes bad, your money is gone. However, the risk is only $1,000. The chances of a company which came out of reorganization going down is slim, but the stock can easily drop if there's an earthquake in Arizona. Natural disasters can have bearish effects on the most bullish stock. How does one guard against this risk?

For the trader who has large amounts of capital another avenue is open to reduce market risks: hedge trading. Simply, it involves simultaneous entering long and short positions in different stocks. For every long position entered in one stock, a short position must be entered in another stock. In this manner the larger trader is immunized against market risk and concentrates on the individual strengths or weaknesses of the stocks which he positions. (Large Commodity Trading Advisors use futures contracts instead of stocks as their investment vehicles; similarly, bond traders use different maturities of their bonds.)

An assassination of a political leader or an earthquake which destroys a financial center will have no market risk effect on the large trader's net positions. The long positions will drop as much as the short positions. The net effect will be the same. He loses $20 each share on the long stock, but he makes back $20 each share on each short stock. Result: zero loss or profit. Yet,

147

through the correct application of technical decision-making tools, the trader is long the strongest stock and short the weakest stock. He makes money in this manner; but he doesn't lose money to market risk.

Having successfully neutralized market risk as it affects his portfolio the large trader can now put more capital to work. This hedge concept approach is now a monstrous juggernaut which ingests unlimited capital and excretes neatly packaged but matched (in many senses) long/short market risk pairs of stocks.

Because of the large amount of capital they have at their disposal to trade and invest in markets the hedgers' basic strategy mitigates against unforecastable events; one countertrend position acts as an insurance hedge against the possibility that these events can and do occur.

For example, if the large trader has already picked the two stocks he wants to be both long and short, he must put those two trades on. How does he go about doing it? He works the more difficult of the two stocks first. Once he has that side done, then he goes to the other side which is the more liquid. Let's say he has decided to buy IBM stock and short Digital Equipment stock as the paired hedge stock. IBM is considerably more liquid than Digital Equipment. He executes his position in Digital Equipment first, and then goes to execute his IBM side. When it comes time to unwind the position, he repeats the same strategy: execute the less liquid stock first, then close the transaction by doing the more liquid side.

The strategy is not as simplistic as this chapter implies because, like anything else in life, the actual application of any concept always brings unforeseen problems. Other nuances and eye-opening problems can occur when you implement these strategies to take advantage of huge amounts of capital. This chapter has explained only the core concept of reducing market risk.

RULE 34

NOTHING NEW EVER OCCURS IN THE MARKETS

History repeats itself. So what else is new? What's new is that the manner in which history repeats itself is of significance in attempting to forecast future events.

Most speculators are too tied into the markets to see the stages of the markets they are in. They cannot see similarities in different situations, and they cannot extrapolate what they have observed into other situations. Markets are always repeating, in some form or another, what occurred in the past. But because the actual suggestions and implications are different, market players often overlook what they saw in the past and close their minds to nuances that can be important to a correct analysis of the current situation.

Creativity is important in the forecasting process because it helps you use previous situations to form another possible scenario. In thinking about how current conditions reflect what transpired in the past, it is necessary to know that not everything will be repeated exactly. Certain conditions will repeat, but others will not; some new conditions might come to the forefront.

In forecasting future events, there are three time brackets to consider: past, present, and future. It is beyond the scope of this chapter to discuss random walk and how it relates to market prices. Depending upon the time span of your analysis, it is possible to accept the random walk theory and at the same time to accept trending markets. If your market action analysis is based on a defined time span, and if you lengthen the time

149

span, you will see the validity of the random walk theory, but if you define your time frame to be progressively more discrete time intervals, you will see that you can forecast imminent price moves.

There are two types of thinkers who are active in the markets: forward thinkers and backward thinkers. Each group has its strengths, but only one excels in current markets.

Forward thinkers take past events and actions, input current actions, and arrive at a prospective scenario for the future. They use the backdrop of past events and current action to create an outline on which future forecasts can be fleshed out.

Backward thinkers also take past action, input new action, and look for past scenarios to repeat in the future. However, backward thinkers, as the name implies, are forever looking backwards. They do not add that extra consciousness in their thinking to accommodate more varied future projections.

For the last decade or so, many doomsday economists have been forecasting their own brands of Armageddon. I must admit that I once advocated a cleansing of the world's economic machinery through inflation-depression cycles, which were highly touted, both in the West and the Soviet East, but I was not as extreme as most modern day survivalists.

To illustrate how the critical differences in thinking can lead to incorrect analysis, I've analyzed past events centered on the Great Depression.

The economic conditions of the world back in the 1930s were dramatically different from today's. In the 1930s there was a developing steel industry and a new automobile manufacturing industry that was a consolidation of many smaller manufacturers. The United States economy was not nearly as deep as it is now. Now, the automobile industry itself generates enough gross annual sales to match the gross national product of a lesser developed country. The construction industry is so pervasive in the economy that it is a virtual lumbering giant with such bulk that it takes a long time for it to stop completely or start up again. Each sector of the construction industry can stand by itself and can represent a huge proportion of a smaller country's yearly budgetary expense.

150

Because the different sectors of the United States economy are so huge in absolute numbers, the momentum needed to get each sector going after a standstill or to cause it to come to a standstill is great. In the 1930s it didn't take much for the stock market to col-

> *What we saw over the last 15 years can be classified as a "rolling depression."*

lapse. (This is not to say that there weren't aspects of the overheated stock market back then that made it vulnerable to a major collapse, such as indiscriminate short selling and futures-type margining of stocks.) Since the depth of the economy back then was so superficial, it didn't take long for the economy to collapse after the bulwark stock market dropped.

Today, margin requirements in the stock market are considerably higher, and short selling occurs only on up-ticks. Even though recent innovations such as standardized options trading on exchanges have circumvented the short selling limitations of the stock market itself, there are other safeguards built into the system that prevent the wholesale collapse of individual sectors of the economy.

What is unfolding now is that there has been a depression, of sorts, that has affected the United States economy. Each sector of the economy has taken its respective hit. Since the late 1970s there has been drastic downsizing of various sectors of the economy. The steel industry, which once employed more than 500,000 workers in the mid-1950s saw drastic downsizing and a series of industry shakeouts. At the nadir of the industry's depression, we saw United States Steel Company, once the premier world producer of steel, move out of the steel industry and become an energy producer. Now, the steel industry employs about 50,000 workers in the United States. With a leaner industry, any upturn in business translates into record profits.

In the automobile industry, we recently saw record earnings from Chrysler and Ford Motors. Before that, we saw depressed conditions cause Chrysler to downsize when it sold its tank division and cut back drastically on plant expansions, American Motors to seek a European partner, and Ford Motors to invest heavily in capital plant expansions. Monolithic General Motors has had extremely good sales, but it is a monolith. The depression that hit the automobile industry forced major repositioning of key players.

In the construction industry, we saw commercial and residential properties top out in the late 1970s. Since then, after the rolling series of depression-like conditions affecting it, real estate has been making selective rallies. The single-family home markets have moved to new high prices, aided by government policies primarily through the retention of tax deductions and the removal of tax shelters in commercial properties. In most areas of the United States, commercial properties have not regained their previous highs. The government knows that its bread and butter comes from taxpayers, so it has maintained the residential mortgage interest deductions.

Throughout the 10 to 15 years during which we saw such gyrations in the individual sectors, the United States economy found support in other sectors that had bottomed out earlier or were on intermediate rallies.

What we saw over the last 15 years can be classified as a "rolling depression." The depression of the 1930s was an individualized depression. In the 1930s, your neighbor got laid off. The depression of the 1980s and 1990s is an *institutionalized* depression. In the 1980s, whole sectors of the economy got work stoppages. Back in the 1930s home mortgages did not allow continual amortizations of the principal. Interest payments were made; and, at the end of the mortgage life, a lump sum for the equity of the home was paid. In the 1980s, monthly home payments include an amortization of principal, small though it might be. Today, lending institutions are feeling the squeeze even more than homeowners.

RULE 35

Money Cannot Be Made Every Day From the Markets

When I first started out as a trader at the MidAmerica Commodity Exchange, I made money on a very erratic basis. One day I would make several hundred dollars and the next I would lose several hundred dollars. On balance, I made a positive amount of money, but it was difficult to know what the accounting period was. If the accounting period was monthly, then I would have streaks of months where I made money and streaks where I lost money. This made for an extremely erratic cash flow, yet the expenses were steady and unrelenting.

The problem was compounded by the fact that the prior job I had was at the First National Bank of Chicago in the early 1970s. I was still living at home and had been spoiled by a steady paycheck. The monthly equation was always balanced:

$$\text{Income} = \text{Expenses} + \text{Savings}.$$

As a single person with no obligations, any money I made, I saved or invested in stocks. Before starting my independent career as a floor trader, I had accumulated enough savings to acquire a MidAm membership at $4,600 and to open a trading account for $3,000. As I devoted more time to futures trading, I learned to adjust to erratic income. It took several years for me to realize that the few markets I traded did not present profit situations every day.

There are three types of members and three basic types of trading they can participate in:

- Scalping members—scalp for minimum ticks
- Day trading members—day trade for intermediate moves
- Long-term trading members—position for long-term moves

Most members switch back and forth in trading styles, but outside traders can only use day trading and long-term trading with any effectiveness. The factors that affect the availability of trading styles are commission costs and ease of executions.

Scalping Daily for Profits

All scalping is done in one market at one point in time. I have seldom found successful scalpers in more than one market during a trading day.

A member of the exchange incurs relatively light commission costs. As of this writing, a member of the Chicago Board of Trade, when executing for his or her own account, pays about $1.50 for a round turn commission and about 25 cents in additional fees and charges. For a round turn trade, the member pays less than $2. If the round turn is done at the same price, it is considered a scratch trade and the commission is merely 10 cents.

A minimum tick in financial futures contracts is $31.25. If the scalper makes a tick profit on one scalp, he or she can afford to make about 312 scratch trades and still wind up at breakeven for the day. As long as the minimum tick is considerably greater than the cost of around turn commission, the member who is a scalper can make a decent living scalping for minimum ticks.

Scalpers on the floor have extremely high commission bills. A friend who scalps at the Chicago Board Options Exchange has paid as much as $30,000 a month for member's commissions. The clearing firms prize these clients very much. Around Christmas time, they sometimes make their gratitude known by giving such clients $20,000 Cadillacs. Several clearing firms have condominiums in Hawaii, Florida, and Colorado available for the use of these members.

As members, scalpers are shown the public orders coming into the pit. They can take advantage of this information in the process of scalping into tick profit or loss situations. During a single trading session, the scalper can take positions in as many as 10,000 contracts, always looking to make a tick profit at best, a tick loss at worst, or a scratch at a breakeven.

Unfortunately, I am inclined to be a thinker. I found out early in my career that scalping offered a steady income, but it was a lot of work. Laziness was not the problem; I just felt more comfortable thinking out my plays rather than sweating for tick profits by trading 2,000 contracts every day. This attitude has not endeared me to the clearing firms. I remember telling the principal of a firm that I had made $700 on a 1-lot of bond futures. He didn't seem happy because his firm only made $2 on my trade.

> *It is possible for the retail trader to make money on a daily basis in a few markets from a portfolio of many markets; there is still no guarantee, but the chances of making money are better.*

Members who scalp have four basic advantages over the market and the retail public: (1) No capital is required to hold overnight positions, when dramatic news can move markets adversely against the trader. (2) Liquidity in the pits as public orders come in allows members to enter and exit the market with minimum losses. (3) Commission costs are less than the minimum ticks in all traded markets. (4) Scalping requires no real market analysis.

Scalping is not economically possible for nonmembers, largely because of commission costs. If a retail trader is charged in excess of $50 for a roundturn commission, that trader cannot break even on a scratch trade. A retail trader loses money on a scratch as well as a loss, can only make money if the trade is a winner, and has to have a series of tick scalp winners to make consistent money.

If the commissions were brought down to less than the minimum tick, retail traders would have a better chance of making profits, but that's not a chance I would take. If a retail trader uses the services of a discount brokerage firm that charges about $20 for a roundturn execution and the trader makes a tick profit ($31.25 in the case of bond futures), he or she winds up with a net profit of $11.25 less other fees. The retail trader can now afford to scratch only 0.5625 times on the next series of trade ($11.25 profit divided by $20), which is impossible since fractions of trades cannot be executed. Note that the retail trader can scratch only 0.5625 times, whereas in a similar tick profit situation, the scalping member can afford to scratch 312 times. The member has a 555 times advantage: 312/0.5625.

Day Trading for Profits

Once you move away from scalping, you will have a better chance to make money on a consistent basis, if you know how to create and handle your own risk opportunities.

If the market you are trading has a relatively large daily range, it is possible to day trade it for a profit, but not necessarily on a daily basis. Commissions are a serious disadvantage to the retail trader. In the case of the scalper we saw a member of the exchange who was as willing to take a tick loss as to take a tick profit. A day trading retail trader is willing to take many ticks profits as well as many ticks losses; he or she tries to minimize the losses while squeezing as many ticks as possible on the profit side.

Since the day trader, whether a member or an outside trader, is willing to take many more ticks losses to assure that he or she is in a position to take many more ticks profits, the capital needed to sustain these plays must be greater than a scalper's capital. The increased capital is required not because the traders will be carrying positions overnight, but because they are positioning during the course of the day. Once traders start to lengthen the timeframe of their market risk, more capital is required to insure against market risk. In the case of the scalper, there was practically no long-term market risk: The scalper was out of the position on the next trade and in on another position on the next one.

Even with this increased potential to make larger profits, there is no assured way to obtain daily profits as a day trader. However, the scene is now set so that retail traders have increasing advantages over the scalping floor members. What was once a slight advantage to floor scalpers—that they scalp daily in only one market to maximize liquidity and centralization of orders—now proves to be a tremendous disadvantage if they try to day trade. Because the retail traders are not tied to one market in making their trades, they can watch several markets and trade opportunities that present themselves on a daily basis.

It is possible for the retail trader to make money on a daily basis in a few markets from a portfolio of many markets that he is trading. There is still no guarantee, but the chances of making money are better. Unfortunately, along with increased opportunities for profitable daily day trading also comes the potential to position into losing situations due to poor market analysis. The losing plays can offset the winners. Again, you have to be careful about trying to generate money daily, even if you are watching more markets.

Long-term Trading for Profits

As we lengthen the time frame for trading, we are discovering that the advantage of exchange membership is the ability to scalp markets. If the markets you are trading have enough daily movements over the range, then it can be profitable to trade on a daily basis if there are enough such opportunities. To increase such opportunities, you must track more markets.

Of the three types of traders we have defined so far, long-term traders have the greatest control of market risks. Because they take the longest viewpoint of market movement, these traders have the greatest number of profitable market situations available to them. The scalper has access to the orders going into the pit, but when the volume in that market diminishes, so does the scalper's advantage.

Long-term traders must also have the greatest capital base to work from. Since their approach is to find profitable situations and position themselves for expected moves, long-term traders do not trade every day as a scalper or a day trader with a large portfolio would. Rather, they accumulate large positions for longer duration moves. This means they need enough capital to cover margins and margin calls as a result of temporary setbacks and to cover their living expenses while waiting for the profitable moves to unfold.

The long-term trading approach is the most amenable to retail traders in terms of risk exposure, assuming that they have the capital to sit with losing positions for a long time. However, the long-term trader of such proportions is often a member of the exchanges. In order to take such huge positions, a long-term trader has to specialize in a few markets. An expert in such markets would find it advantageous to be a member of an exchange.

Professional traders know that they cannot make money every day. The money they make today could be lost tomorrow, so they adjust their expenses to accommodate erratic income flows. All traders recognize an inherent weakness with trading for profits: If you don't trade you don't make money. Hence, it is incumbent on the traders to trade every day. However, this isn't the way to make profits. Instead, traders should trade more on profit opportunities.

RULE 36

NARROWNESS ALWAYS FOLLOWS A VIOLENT MARKET MOVE; THUS, WHEN STOCKS, "MARK TIME," YOU DO THE SAME

One of the most boring things to do is to watch paint dry. I haven't actually sat down to watch paint dry, but at times life resembles this slow waiting. You've got to watch and wait. Wait and watch. Any combination of permutation, but not act!

The markets are often the most boring things to watch. Right now as I write this chapter, the Dow Jones Industrial Averages have been in a tight range of about 75 points for the last month. Boring. It looks like I'm watching oil-based enamel paint drying. It wouldn't be so boring had it been quick-drying latex paint.

Prior to this period of "marking time" of the market, the market dropped from a high of 4,000 to a bit under 3,600 in about a five-month period. Some stocks dropped over 50 percent in value. Very few gained in value. A majority are down between 10–15 percent from their high prices.

Yet, as I watch the market chew around at this level, I've kept myself busy both within the markets by doing more research and outside by writing more books. This prevents my nerves from getting to me and playing games with my perception of reality.

> *In the case of options, to take advantage of the waiting periods, you sell premium and at the same time take on positions which will mitigate your risk, in case you are wrong on the options you have sold.*

Why is this so and what can we do about this? What mind games must we play with ourselves to insure that we don't give back what profits we have accumulated? First, you must transfer an observation you have seen in real life: for every action there is a reaction to the marketplace.

Markets move up. They move down. They go sideways or nowhere. There are no other patterns. Given these three types of market action, all interconnected and interrelated with each other in an ongoing continuum of market activity, you should know when to get into the market or stay out of it. Of course, there are strategies and plays that involve getting into the market plays when most other players are out! These sets of strategies involve options, and I'll discuss the role of the option player later.

When a market moves dramatically from one price level to another, the market must need time to settle down. In the process of moving from one price level to another the market has upset the balance of ownership. Those who bought stock at $100 are selling on the way down. When the stock hits a low enough level where active sellers are sold out, the market will rest and stabilize while the rest of the market players regroup and reassess their damage or profits. At $50 a share there are those who still own the stock at $100. If they haven't sold out at $100, they were surely selling on the way down. The market moved down to a level where all those who were holders of less conviction had already bailed out.

Now at $50 a share, the new price level itself attracts newer buyers into the markets to support the price, i.e., prevent the price from going lower at least on a temporary basis.

The early sellers were either sharp traders or else they had been buyers on margin and they needed to get out based on margin calls. Less frequently will appear sellers at $50. There is a small group of short sellers at this level. Whether or not they are profitable shorts is unknown by this type of market action. I can say with assurance that anyone shorting on the relative low of the move must either know something about the company or else is totally misinformed.

Once the ownership of stock changes hands at the $50 level, the price may or may not go back up. This all depends on the intrinsic value and the fundamental bullishness of the particular stock. In certain situations, the general tone of the market, either bullish or bearish, will be reflected in the majority of stocks going up or down. This particular $50 stock may be prone to the general movement of the market.

After the dramatic selloff comes the dull waiting period. Bullish forces must regroup to take the stock back up. Remember also that this resumption to the upside must take a longer time than it took for it to go down because the price territory from which the stock came—higher than $50—has left a lot of owners of the stock still "holding the bag." From $50 back up to $100 the strong bullish forces will encounter sellers. This is the additional reason why the stock must boringly build a base at the $50 level. The market has no other way to take out the "overhead" supply of stock from buyers and owners of the stock at higher prices. Until this supply is absorbed the stock will have a hard time going back up.

Many games can be played on the holders of the longs while prices are at such low levels. Bad news may be coming out about the company to panic these owners into dumping out their longs. Rumors may be flying of the company going under. The best strategy to shake ownership out of the hands of these losing investors is to allow their own fears to work on their nerves: let time pass without any news.

The informed speculator will look particularly at the base building for clues that there is "rotation" of ownership. By reading the tape and watching the bids and asks, the speculator can discern when the informed buying shows itself more. Buying and selling are occurring during the base building, but as an informed speculator you want to see ownership of stock shift from bits and pieces to block buyers. The assumption is that block buyers are more intelligent traders and when they buy the prices will eventually go up.

The expectation is that after a base-building period prices have a better than even chance of going back up. The resumption to the upside may or may not take out new highs, but the trader will observe noticeable movement to the upside.

So when prices are steady after a runup or a selloff, you must observe to see when the respective selling or buying increases steadily. Once you see this happen, you can mathematically presume that the price will reverse direction and you can get on board for the capital gains.

Note: in the case of options, you can take advantage of the boring, "waiting" period to your financial advantage. To take advantage of time, you sell premium and at the same time take on positions which will mitigate your risk in case you are wrong on the options you have sold. This is *spreading*. Option spreaders take advantage of the waiting periods by shifting the element of time to their side. Instead of letting time work against them, the spreaders sell options premium short and essentially allow the passage of time to erode the values of these options. In this manner the premium seller will receive the gain on the shorting of the options. At expiration, if all conditions are met (the options are not called away due to the option getting into the money), the premium seller would have gained from the passage of time. The real problem with this type of strategy is that spreading is more complicated, so I do *not* recommend using spreading strategies without additional study.

RULE 37

ARBRITAGE PLAYS ARE EVERYWHERE

There are so many ways to make money in the markets but only a few solid ways to make money consistently. I've found myself in several situations where I was able to exploit a market situation that was topical. Once that area exhausted itself I was forced to look elsewhere since the plays would no longer exist. Still, I suggest that you look outside of the conventional plays to make other opportunities happen.

Arbitrage means the process of buying and selling similar stock, currency, or commodity which is priced differently on different markets. For example, IBM stock is traded both in the United States and in London. If the price of IBM is higher in the United States and lower in London, then the process of arbitrage means the person performing the arbitrage buys the stock in London and sells the stock in the United States and captures the difference between the two prices.

The simplistic arbitrage is the one that everyone knows how to do. The more creative arbitrage situations require more understanding of the mechanics of the markets. The creative arbitrages require considerable research and thoroughness in analysis.

The first example that we'll look at involves a pure stock arbitrage play. The second example also involves an arbitrage play; this is an intermarket play. The third example illustrates and broadens your idea of what an arbitrage should be: a conceptual arbitrage. By leading you through the mental process of stock arbitrage to its broader concept, conceptual arbitrage, I hope to teach you a thinking process which will allow you to make money in all types of markets.

Stock Versus Stock (Like Versus Like)

What would you say if I told you of a market play that costs you absolutely no money? No risk. Nothing. What would you say? Too good to be true? Yes, but some of those plays are around. More often than you would ever believe.

I achieved one of my speculative successes in a company on the verge of bankruptcy. I managed to make a very successful play in it, profits from which I later used to play larger market positions elsewhere.

The company was Chrysler Corporation, which was on the verge of bankruptcy in 1980 when Iacocca was brought in from Ford Motor Corporation to run it.

The play involved something as simple as buying the preferred stock which has equity risk, and shorting the common stock as insurance against the company going bankrupt.

What may surprise you is that for the last 10 or so years Chrysler has not had a preferred stock issue outstanding. The last one issued by the company was in 1978 when it issued a $2.75 cumulative convertible preferred stock, which was callable by 1983 at $25 per share.

Based on information from *Moody's Industrial Manual* (1978), these were the salient details of the issue: On June 20, 1978, 10,000,000 shares were offered by Merrill Lynch White Weld Capital Markets Group, First Boston Corporation and associates. Each unit consisted of $2.75 preferred stock plus one-half warrant on the common stock. Chrysler Corporation $2.75 cumulative preferred with par value of $25. There were 20,000,000 shares authorized but only 10,000,000 outstanding. It had preference rights over the common stock in dividends and assets (a critical component to the arbitrage play). Holders of the preferred were entitled to cumulative cash dividends at the rate of $2.75 per share per year, payable quarterly. In liquidation, holders are entitled to receive $25 per share plus accrued dividends. This was callable on and after July 1, 1983, on at least 30 but not more than 60 days notice at $25 per share plus accrued dividends.

Arbitrage means the process of buying and selling similar stock, currency, or commodity which is priced differently on different markets.

Figure 37.1 shows the price activity of Chrysler common stock from 1974 to 1985. The price range was from a low of $3.125 to a high of about $45 per share. A price chart of the pre-ferred stock is unavailable since no charting service tracked the preferred issues. I was able to obtain the high–low trading ranges from research materials of the preferred stock on a daily basis which validated the arbitrage play.

Once the company's fundamentals turned bad, the play was to buy the Chrysler preferred and short the Chrysler stock. The price of both issues went down to the $3–$4 level. This was true for both stocks! On April 15, 1982, both stocks touched a low of $3 and a fraction. The difference between the two stocks went as low as $0.50, when the common traded at $4.875 and the pre-ferred traded at $5.25.

My strategy rested on the fact that if the Chrysler company went down the tubes then the common stock would be worth-less. At whatever price I shorted the stock it would eventually go to zero upon bankruptcy liquidation. Meanwhile, the Chrysler preferred I bought would also go down. The difference in what I lost on the preferred versus the money I made on the common stock short would be the actual amount I lost. The spread ranged from $2.00 to $0.50; in a worst-case scenario I would lose no more than $2 per spread play. The upside was limited by the price of the preferred stock. The preferred divi-dends, even though they weren't paid out because the company had no earnings, accumulated relentlessly.

As the proceedings to get funding for Chrysler's bailout pro-gressed, it appeared as if Chrysler might be able to come back from the grave. The stock market responded. The price of the common rose. The price of the preferred stock rose faster. The

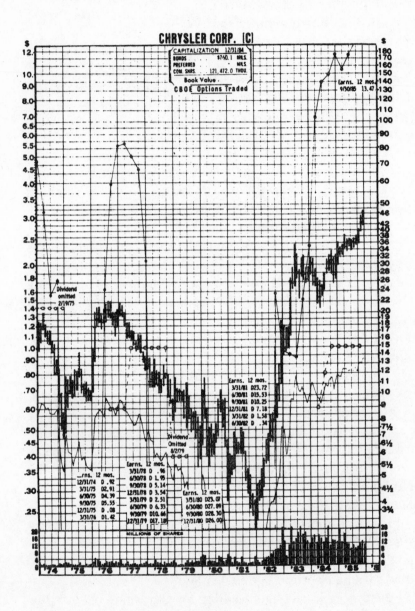

Fig. 37.1   Price activity of Chrysler Corporation stock, 1974–85

widest the difference between the two was about $7.50. At that point in the spread, the preferred had risen to the price of about $25 and the common had risen to about $17–$18.

With the spread having widened from a low of $0.50 to $7.50, I figured it was time to take profits. Within less than two years, the return on this arbitrage play was about 500 percent annualized (1½ years holding period, risk of $0.50 to make $7.50). I can't remember what the cumulated dividends on the preferred were, but it came to a positive carry for the spread play! Yikes, they even paid me to hold the positions!

At the point of unwinding the spread, by buying in the short common at $17.50 and selling the preferred at $25, I, the arbitrageur, could have opted to take the $7 net profit and then buy the common stock for an outright hold with the profits. Instead of buying the full amount of shares, the purchase would have been determined by the net profit: for every spread trade profit of one share I could take the $7 net profit and buy a proportionate share of common.

There is free money in a free position

Watching the common stock rise from this point on is riskless! Chrysler is now trading at around $60 per share, adjusted for splits. That's another 1,000 percent return on the outright position. Once you know how the game on Wall Street is played and how to play it, you can really profit. As a result, the profits from the play further capitalized my trading. Thank you, Chrysler. Thank you, Lee Iacocca.

Stock Versus Similar Value (Like Versus Similar)

The second example of an arbitrage play rests with broadening the concept of arbitraging. To arbitrage stock versus stock isn't necessary! From a conceptual viewpoint, you can arbitrage anything against anything else; the more obviously removed each of these two arbitragable items are from each other, the greater the potential for profit.

The problem rests with attempting to "create a connection" between two presumed arbitrageable items when realistically there aren't any connections. This is one of the reasons why traders are always looking for correlations between items. The first sign of statistically significant correlations—either positively or negatively correlated—indicates a possible connection. There may not be, in fact, any relevance between the arbitrageable items, but traders must heed this first sign. This germinating point is where potentially lucrative trading situations spring forth. Those who can perceive, not see, the correlations can then trade one item against the other before the rest of the trading community gets hold of these ideas.

A legal, profitable arbritrage example from an illegal action

Eastman Kodak developed a line of instant photography cameras years ago by infringing on the patent rights of Polaroid Corporation. For several years, Eastman Kodak manufactured their own cameras and sold their own instant film. One day Polaroid hauled Eastman Kodak into court for violations of Polaroid's instant camera patents. The case dragged on for years and eventually Eastman Kodak lost one of the largest patent infringement lawsuits ever filed. Kodak was ordered to pay $909,000,000 to Polaroid for infringement of five of the latter's patents.

As this was going on a unique arbitrage play was occurring.

The settlement involved reimbursing the owners of instant cameras since Kodak was now no longer able to manufacture the film. The initial reimbursement package came in the form of coupons for processing film, credit toward the purchase of other Kodak cameras and supplies, or a share of stock in Eastman Kodak. As a stock trader I wasn't interested in the film or cameras, but I was interested in the stock.

I didn't own an instant camera but I sensed an arbitrage play here: The announcements came across the broad tape practically every day after Kodak lost the suit in court. So I monitored the outcome.

I did my research on the camera and found Kodak sold a lot of them, but I reasoned that not too many people who bought Kodak cameras were that market savvy. I called up a local discount retail company, McDade (which has since gone bankrupt), and inquired about the instant camera. The inventory manager told me they had 37 new cameras, but had no film for them because they could no longer be manufactured by Kodak. He told me that he would sell them to me at $18 a piece. I'm sure I could have negotiated and taken down the price to about $10 a piece. Why not? Cameras not being made anymore and film production ended. What is a holder of the camera to do? Make his own film so that he can use the camera?

The price of Eastman Kodak stock was trading at a bit above $50 a share. An arbitrage situation of about $50 a share. Not a bad play.

I immediately scoured around the Chicagoland area for more cameras. I wanted to accumulate 100 cameras and convert to 100 shares of stock. The company was giving me $32 a share to take the cameras back to them. Sounded good to me. While doing this halfheartedly, I found 76 more cameras available in the Chicago land area.

Kodak had set up a toll-free line for dealing with inquiries concerning this reimbursement package. I knew where to get my inventory. I called the toll-free line and inquired how many cameras I could bring in. The operator looked in her instruction manual and could find no mention of how many cameras could be brought in by one person or family. They absolutely had no policy in this matter. I started to think of thousands of cameras. If someone paid me $32 for each camera I could locate and return, I'll stand on my head and do it all day. The beauty of what I was doing was that I could do it in batches. One phone call got me an average of 15 cameras? or a quick $480 for ten minutes or less.

And there was no downside risk. I said to the operator I would call back in a month to get updated information.

Then as I was plotting to pick up the cameras, an announcement came across the tape that a camera owner had sued Eastman Kodak for not offering an additional option: repayment in cash. Now why take the darn thing in cash? The stock is just as good as cash and we were still at the beginning stages of a bull market. The stock would appreciate to $70 in no time flat.

Then began a protracted series of legal proceedings. I'm a stock trader and I wanted the stock. Since there were legal problems with this swap, I delayed my acquisition of the Kodak cameras.

As I continued to follow the proceedings, I happened to be browsing in a used clothing store with a friend who collects antique jewelry. He knew what he was looking for and every so often he would find a bargain amidst all the junk jewelry. Then an intriguing opportunity presented itself.

While in the store I happened to find a used Kodak instant film camera. I bought it for $5 and promptly sent it in to Kodak for reimbursement, whenever that would occur.

By this time Kodak had implemented a policy to limit the number of instant cameras that one person or family could return. Imagine my chagrin when I found out that I could return no more than ten cameras! Not worth the time of day for me to play around with this anymore!

I received one of about 3,400,000 checks that Kodak sent out that year. The total cost to Kodak on this portion of the settlement came to about $200,000,000 for all the Kodak instant cameras that were sold and returned to Kodak from 1976 to 1986.

The Eastman Kodak/Polaroid situation was minute, but it thoroughly illustrates an arbitrage play that could have made you money on a small scale.

An additional fallout from Eastman Kodak losing on the patent infringement was that Polaroid eventually raised prices on its own line of products because Kodak was no longer making a competing product. So Polaroid really won twice, once in court and once in the stores.

Idea Versus Idea (Conceptual Arbitrage) or: How to Sell a Newsletter Many Times

I've shown you a conventional arbitrage in the strictest sense of the term—stock versus stock—and one involving stock and non-stock. Now let's look at an arbitrage that's conceptual in nature but which you should be able to extrapolate further into the real world.

I was a regular panelist on one of the local television stations for a brokerage company that sponsored a weekly interview show. Three panelists asked questions of an invited industry expert for each taping. The brokerage company taped guests in batches, often interviewing three guests per taping session.

I arrived several minutes early for the taping of this show and sat in the waiting room. One of the other guests, Dennis Dunn of the money management firm Dunn & Hargitt, had arrived earlier from Indiana. Prior to getting into the money management area they had been publishers of point and figure charts. I knew the reputation of Dunn & Hargitt, so I was a bit awed to be in the same sitting room with this man who was a partner in the firm.

As we were waiting for our taping we engaged in conversation. I always like to find out what people's backgrounds are, to understand where they are coming from. Dennis Dunn was a pleasant person, nonobtrusive and very congenial. He was classy.

The conversation delved into the early beginnings of the Dunn & Hargitt Company. Dunn told me they hadn't always been involved in the markets. They were first a publisher of a monthly newsletter on child development. Their company published a monthly newsletter which was sent out every month to subscribers who were raising children.

I asked Dunn how they got the names to solicit directly. He told me they would find lists of newborns from hospitals and solicit their families in a direct mail piece on the benefits of subscribing to their child development newsletter.

I commented that writing a newsletter was very tough work. I mumbled to Dennis Dunn that he had to block out two weeks for each issue, so I sympathized with him on the amount of work that had to go into each and every issue of the newsletter.

171

Dunn replied that he had no more work to do. At this point he said all he had to do was this: market the newsletter, fill the subscription order, and bill the subscribers. I was puzzled. I asked him whether or not he hired people to write the newsletter, and he said no and that he and his earlier associates were the ones who wrote the newsletters. I was even more puzzled. Then he proceeded to explain to me what he had done so he now no longer needed to write the newsletter.

Here was a newsletter publisher who never had to write a newsletter any more! Another paradox in life!

In the early development of the newsletter he and his partners had created each issue from scratch. This was the hardest part. Each issue detailed to the parents what they could expect from their developing babies. One month separated the issues. So, the first issue was for a one-month old baby; the second month's issue was for a two-month old baby, and so forth.

Once their company had created this inventory of newsletters, they had everything they needed. This set of newsletters then had to be marketed. The products were there! All they needed to do was to find a newborn to a new set of parents and essentially sell them the newsletter "series." When a baby was one-month old Dunn pulled out the master for the one-month newsletter and sent it. When the baby was two months old, Dunn pulled out the second newsletter, made a copy of it, and sent it out. This went on until the child became an adolescent. (For a detailed write-up about this see "Starting Your Own Newsletter," by Berkeley Rice *Money Magazine*, March 1984.)

Were was the arbitrage situation here, you might ask? It's a bit more difficult to perceive in this example because it is more subtle, but it is distinctly an arbitrage. But this example will allow you to make yourself if a millionaire, if you can find a similar arbitrage situation.

This is how the arbitrage situation worked. There are two entities: the newsletter series and the new baby. The newsletter series had been created earlier and all the knowledge on the development of a baby was encompassed in its pages. To the baby, everything at the time of birth was completely new— "new" desires, needs, demands, etc. But what is new to the

172

baby and the parents isn't really new. From the perspective of the information contained in the newsletter, nothing was new; in fact, it could be considered old information, but it's new to each new mom and dad.

Dunn had managed to "leg" into a time-based spread which is another way to look at an arbitrage situation. The elegance of this situation entailed no open market risk! He was long the "infinite time" side and picked and chose his time sensitive side to offset against. The infinite time side was the set of newsletters; this product seldom, if ever, aged. The physical, mental, and emotional development of the child were encompassed within the pages of the newsletter. The children to fit into this developmental mode were constantly being born, always going through these stages of development, which were naturally found in the newsletters. This was brilliant!

At any moment in time, the newborn, had he or she known it, could have asked Dunn for copies of the newsletter from future editions or even from past editions. At the age of six the newborn could have read what he was to be like at the age of 15! At any moment in time, the newborn had access to information from the past and the future! But because the newborn was not aware of this, and most likely neither were the parents, no such foreknowledge was available.

From other people's broader experiences, the concept of knowing the future is possible and highly probable because the past, present, and future exist now! This example is simplistic, but the concept is the same: this is an example of forecasting. The markets have already been etched out in stone. To be able to accurately "forecast" them, like the newsletter writer who found the right newsletter to send at the right time in the baby's life, we merely have to find the right model to base our forecasts.

How can you extend this conceptual arbitrage into your real life? Start by looking for situations which are similar to the Eastman Kodak/Polaroid situation. Once you see how this works, then you can move the concept of arbitrage completely out of the stock realm and into real life which this child development newsletter pointed out.

RULE 38

BACK YOUR OPINIONS WITH CASH WHEN THEY ARE CONFIRMED BY MARKET ACTION

There are several ways to enter the markets and make money. You can either play the market for a one-directional move and look to get on board a move when it does occur; or you can anticipate a move and position yourself ahead of time for this type of market action. Depending on the capital and resources you have on hand, you can implement strategies to take advantage of either of these scenarios.

Anticipatory markets are ones that you position ahead of time. Heavily capitalized traders and investors trade markets in this manner because they have resources that are not available to smaller investors and speculators. One such resource is research to allow them to analyze and anticipate ultimate trend reversals. Another resource they have is enough capital to position well ahead of an ultimate trend reversal. However, one of the ironies of having so much capital is the fact that they must anticipate market reversals.

The fact that markets can trade in units ranging from one contract to several thousand contracts shows that both small and large traders are playing the markets. Small traders have different needs and different advantages than larger traders. Small traders have no liquidity problem in most markets because they do not trade positions large enough to affect price movements to any extent. Larger traders, on the other hand, have enough capital that if they position themselves in one stock or commodity, they can actually move the price against the intermediate trend.

The difference between a small trader and a large one was shown to me many years ago by Harold Goodman, a very successful trader at the MidAmerica Commodity Exchange.

One day I was trading silver in the pit, and my analysis showed a bullish scenario. In bull markets, the strategy was to buy the breakouts to the upside. The first day I saw the markets go through new highs, I immediately bought several contracts. The problem with my strategy was that I was buying the breakouts to the upside all the time only to see the prices back off to somewhere around the middle of the previous trading range. As a scalper I sat with a long position in a bull market retracement. Because I was not heavily capitalized, I couldn't stay with the losses, so I managed to sell out at the bottom of the reaction. I continued to do this for several weeks, always sustaining losses.

> *Small traders have different needs and advantages than larger traders. Small traders have no liquidity problem in most markets because they do not trade positions large enough to affect price movements to any extent.*

Finally, I gave up and sat back away from the pit area just watching the markets make new highs. What was the problem with my approach? I was long in a bull market that was making new highs, yet I always got kicked out of my positions on retracements.

I went back into the pit and started buying breakouts on new highs; again and again I got hurt. One day I looked over and saw Harold Goodman walking into the pit. This was the first time I had ever seen him trading silver. I watched how he traded. He did the same things I did. When I bought a new high, he would buy on new highs also. In my case I only bought a few contracts, whereas Harold was buying hundreds. Day after day, Harold would talk about the money he made with his position from the previous day. In my case, I lost money day after day by executing the same trading strategy.

After losing a good chunk of my equity, I finally asked Harold what he was doing that was making him so much money. I bought when he bought, yet I had lost a lot of money doing exactly what he was doing. He leaned over to me and whispered that the difference between his position and my position was that he was already long in silver when he bid up the new highs. At the new highs he was only *adding* to his total position, which was partially obtained at much lower prices. He pointed out that I was right in being long, as anyone should be in bull markets, but that I was initiating new positions at the probable immediate highs of the moves. At the beginning of the day's trading, I was flat.

The difference between my trading and Harold's is like the difference between a large speculator and a small one. Harold was able to add to positions that he had already in place. In my case, I should have traded more on anticipation than actual breakouts because of the lack of capital in my account. Harold was playing for a longer-term perspective. He could afford to buy the new highs because he was only adding on to a larger total position.

RULE 39

A GOOD TRADE IS PROFITABLE RIGHT FROM THE START

How do you know that the trade you entered is a good one? When the trade starts to show a profit. When you buy a stock or futures contract, you are indicating that the price you are paying now is lower than what it will beat a later period.

During the course of the trading day, the price of your stock might fluctuate above and below what you paid for it. The momentary losses are noise inherent in any market action. Do you consider this noise to be a part of your profit analysis?

There is noise in all markets. The unfortunate problem in this day of computerized trading is that we can define more discrete time, price, and volume intervals. Years ago, we analyzed market action based on weekly and monthly charts; now we work with daily and hourly time intervals. As computing power increases, the intervals of market analysis can be reduced even further. We eventually will have the capacity to analyze market action in fractions of seconds. Along with the capacity to analyze market action based on more discrete intervals of analysis comes the problem of defining losses and profits.

When markets were analyzed using weekly and monthly charts, the risks given for each market situation were broader than they are now. If the price of a $30 stock traded in a $5 range on the weekly charts, market strategists allowed a risk factor of about $5, but seldom less. That is, they allowed the price to go against them by about $5 before they started to worry that their analysis might have been wrong. As the intervals of market analysis lessened to daily, the stock was found to have a $2 daily trading range, so the analysts would decrease the risk from $5 to $2. With each decreasing interval, the risk in each trade was reduced to reflect the decreasing range of prices.

> *If a trade you put on shows an immediate loss, you either bought at the high of the move or you bought in a downtrending market.*

The situation now allowed market analysts and traders to reduce their capital exposure by reducing the intervals of analysis. In the process, something was lost in the analysis of market action. Instead of seeing major trends developing in market movements, where a good portion of the money is made in speculation, traders now saw ticks. Instead of living for the long term, they traded for the short term.

With short-term analysis, the definition of profits and losses were correspondingly changed. Instead of looking for a $10 profit in a long-term stock trade, the trader looks for day trading profits of 25¢ in a quick scalp. The problem is that in reducing their intervals they forgot to adjust their losses to 25¢ per trade. Their losses remained at $10 per trade while their profits dipped to 25¢ per trade.

A practical approach would be to limit your risk exposure to the same level as your profit potential. If you trade long-term for $10 profits, make sure that your potential loss is no greater than $10. The ideal situation, however, would be a variation of this. If you trade long-term, do not limit your profits at all, but still maintain a $10 potential loss. In a more discrete time frame, if you want to trade for huge profits, do not limit your profits, but maintain a 25-cent potential loss.

Going back to the original rule of this chapter, where we minimally identified what losses should be relative to profit potentials, you will see that profitable trades always start out as winners and can wind up as losers, depending on the perspective you allot for the trade. Unprofitable trades may or may not start out as winners.

If a trade you put on shows an immediate loss, you either bought at the high of the move or you bought in a downtrending market. If your trade shows an immediate profit, either you bought on the low of the swing or else it had the strength to go up higher than where you bought it. In either case, the price will continue to move in your favor. A trade that initially shows a profit will have a tendency to continue to show a profit.

If you are a floor trader, then when it backs away and shows losses, you must look at the loss in the same frame of reference as your profits. If you are a day trader, the same caution holds: View the loss in the same dimension as your profit potentials.

RULE 40

As Long as a Market is Acting Right, Don't Rush to Take Profits

Many times in my earlier years of trading I carried profitable positions for several days or weeks. Then suddenly, without warning, I got an "urge to purge" and liquidated all my profitable positions. I often had to cash out profitable positions to pay the rent, telephone bill, utility bills, or whatever was more pressing at the time. Regrets ensued when the positions I liquidated continued to make profits . . . for someone else.

Richard Dennis, trader extraordinaire, realized the need for capital to trade larger positions, so he cut his expenses to the bone by removing all need to spend profits. His close friends observed that when he had accumulated well over $500,000 in net worth in his early twenties, he still had not spent any money for a new pair of pants. Traders who visited his apartment in the early years observed that his living room had hardly any furniture except a stack of *Wall Street Journals*. Everybody sat on the papers or empty crates. The money he made in the markets he plowed back into the markets selectively, but with ever-increasing positions.

The market moves up with no regard for the size of your positions, so why not take advantage of it by positioning with right numbers suitable to your trading equity?

After my trading career progressed to the point where I was able to make a stable income, I found that I had conditioned myself with a wrong set of responses. My conditioning to cash out profitable situations to pay bills also carried over into trading situations when I no longer needed the profits to pay bills. I jumped at the chance to make a tick profit here and there because I had become so used to ringing the register in the past. What was once a correct response to the conditions I was living under was now inappropriate if I wanted to make huge capital gains. Like most unsuccessful traders, I had conditioned myself to the wrong actions. Cashing out early is never the right way to make huge capital gains.

> *What you encounter in the real world must not be translated into what the markets are doing to your profitable positions.*

As traders, we are constantly bombarded with situations that demand buy or sell decisions. If the decisions are right, we make money, if the decisions are wrong, we lose money, but we are never at a loss for decision-making opportunities. In fact, we thrive on the opportunity to make more decisions in one day than most people make in a month. It allows us a certain amount of control over our own destiny, microcosmic though it might be. However, we can't get carried away with the decision-making process. Scalping is the only trading role where continuous decision making in the form of executing and closing hundreds of trades on a daily basis is a precondition for success.

The need to experience an adrenaline rush from putting on a trade is not a prerequisite to successful trading. If you are a floor trader and every trade is a physical confrontation with the enemy trader, you need the adrenaline to get you into the "fight or flight" response. These responses have served our ancestors well in their quest for survival. However, in the arena of speculation for profits, constant decision making does not make for successful trading. In fact, constant decision making and the risk arising from increasing frequencies of positions can even expose your trading equity to greater losses.

Think of it this way. When you buy something, you want it to go up. When you sell something, you want it to go down. The chance of entering the trade correctly is small, but the chance of exiting the trade correctly is smaller. The chance of being right on both entering and exiting is the smallest. With such diminishing odds of coming through with a completely correct and, therefore, profitable trading campaign, the fewer decisions you make in the markets, the more profitable your trading should be.

How many people actually get to sell at the top or buy at the bottom? At most, a handful in each reversal area. First, you must be a market follower, once the market has told you what it wants to do. If the market is a raging bull, you have no alternative but to buy. If it is bearish, you have no alternative but to sell every time you get the opportunity. Let the market tell you what to do. To do otherwise is to try to control the markets— something that is only reserved for God and natural disasters. Secondly, selling at the top and buying at the bottom does not guarantee profits. How many times have you heard of traders who managed to sell near the highs or buy near the bottoms, only to miss the ensuing move completely. Instead of making a full swing's profits, they managed to make only several ticks before they closed out their positions.

When you position comfortably into a profitable position, eliminate reasons that are not market-generated and might force you out of it. Find other sources to pay your rent, utility bills, or telephone bills. What you encounter in the real world must not be translated into what the markets are doing to your profitable positions. If you do, you won't be in the business for long if the markets turn choppy and more difficult to trade.

If you are long in the markets and are showing a profit, but you suddenly have an urge to get rid of your winners without any acceptable market-generated reason, execute only one type of trade as a stop-gap measure. Not selling out longs isn't an action, but a passive response. A positive action would be to execute a trade that will add to your position. This will satisfy your need for market action without giving up your winner.

Another way to force yourself to stick with winners is to look elsewhere to initiate plays. If you are long in one market that is acting well, try to find another market to play around in if you have the need for market action. Diversification of assets and equity inadvertently createst his escape valve response. Diversify and look at more market opportunities elsewhere to avoid tampering with your winners.

Once you have initiated a trade that starts to act like a winner, use stop orders to protect your profits and cut your losses. Protecting profits and cutting losses are two entirely different actions. Once your stop orders are correctly placed, you won't have any need to tamper with the position.

Making or losing money is a very emotional subject to deal with and we all bring a different set of parameters to trading because of this. Some of us use the markets to work out hostilities in our everyday lives, often with disastrous results. Treat trading as a business and you will learn to treat the wins and losses in the market place with more detachment.

The only way to make money in the market is to nurture winning positions. If you liquidate your winners, you will never have the opportunity to watch them make more money for you. The other strategy of getting rid of winners and using your capital to look for other winners is not a good one because every time you take on a new position you are taking on new market risks. If you have a winner, nurture it and it will grow into bigger profits.

Nurturing positions that will only break even is a waste of time and the time value of money. Losing positions definitely do not make money. Attention to losers is important because it protects your trading capital. No capital, no more trading.

RULE 41

NEVER PERMIT SPECULATIVE VENTURES TO TURN INTO INVESTMENTS

This rule started as two separate rules, but the second rule, "Money lost by speculation is small compared to money lost in investments," contained many of the same points covered in this chapter. In fact, I have found that in the markets everything is so interrelated that it is very hard to make strong dichotomies of two ideas. Some aspect of any idea is related to another idea.

This is why it is so difficult to become a proficient trader in a short period of time. All trading ideas must be understood in totality at any one point in time, yet each fragmented idea can stand by itself. Complete mastery of individual principles of successful trading often gives you a false belief that you can trade successfully. In fact, you are only able to trade successfully under the limited market conditions then prevailing. If conditions change, as they often do to accommodate changing influences, you would be like a ship without a rudder—floating aimlessly.

There is often muddled thinking when you put on investments and speculations. The inability to define what type of trading you do will result in large loses and continued future bad trading habits. Are you a speculator or are you an investor?

Although so many concepts in the market are interrelated, you must be able to differentiate between investments and speculations. They differ in terms of objectives, time duration, and the amount of capital involved.

Speculation comes from the Latin word, *speculare*, which means "to observe." Speculation involves taking chances on ventures that could turn into profitable situations. You go into speculations knowing that you might lose all your capital. Investment involves using your capital for income or profit. Investments try to provide revenues, whereas in speculation, the primary play is capital gains. Of the two, investments are of a longer duration.

> *Speculation involves taking chances on ventures that could turn into profitable situations. You go into speculations knowing that you might lose all your capital.*

Experienced traders never mix the two approaches. They have conditioned themselves to discriminate what type of approach to use in different market situations. Unsuccessful traders cannot discriminate differences in market situations. They will often trade long term with situations that can only provide quick speculator's profits are invest in speculative positions when market conditions do not warrant holding positions for longer than a day. Those who cannot define the current market, cannot manage the risks it will present. They will get embroiled in market situations over which they have no control and are sure to lose money.

Investments and speculations also differ in terms of time duration: short-term or long-term. As mentioned earlier, speculators are looking for quick profits without much regard for fundamental valuations. In fact, fundamentals are used only to isolate undervalued or overvalued market prices. Once the position is established, the trader seeks to equalize the temporary price and valuation disparity

Investors, on the other hand, respect fundamentals. They regard minor price fluctuations as noise action revolving around a central valuation price that can increase or decrease. Instead of looking for instant market price revaluation due to temporary aberrations, investors look to have the fundamentals unfold over longer time periods.

This discussion of time duration and market analysis approaches brings to mind the age-old debate over which school of analysis is more appropriate—fundamental or technical.

The answer is that both are appropriate at different price levels of the markets. At low prices, fundamentals are more important in helping to determine whether or not to accumulate positions. (Please note that I say "accumulate" positions, not "liquidate.") At low prices, the profit to be made is limited by the fact that prices cannot get below zero. To be absurd, this is a stop loss order at a price of zero.

Technical analysis is more appropriate for high-priced issues or futures. Price action is so volatile at the upper end of prices that there must be more emphasis on liquidating long positions or, for the more speculative trader, on shorting particular markets. Once price moves away from high levels, they move violently away. Fundamentals may correctly account for bearish price action, but by the time correct fundamental analysis is made, price would have moved much too far away for the trader to capitalize on such information.

> *Investment involves using your capital for income or profit. Investments try to provide revenues, whereas in speculation, the primary play is capital gains.*

This type of phased-in market approach—fundamental or technical—has been the secret of success for money managers like John Templeton and Warren Buffet. If they are using fundamental analysis, these managers thrive when markets are moving from an accumulations stage to higher prices. Warren Buffet has even shut down his investment funds when he considered prices to have reached too high a level. With such overvaluation, he cannot find cheap stocks to buy, so he quits the game. John Templeton once thrived on fundamental analysis, but he has modified his approach by integrating arbitrage trading techniques into his investment paradigm. He invests in stocks of foreign countries and moved into currency arbitrage with exchange conversions.

Technical analysts thrive in violently active price action markets. This is why technical analysis is being applied so extensively to the stock market, where price shave quadrupled in the last six years. Technical analysis has always been used in the futures markets, which are subject to violent price actions.

The leveraging factor in futures, where as little as 3 percent of the market valuation of the contract traded can be used to control the other 97 percent, is so great that the most minute relative price move can be reflected in drastic trading account equity drawdowns or increases.

Finally, there is the consideration of the amount of capital required to either speculate or invest. The speculator tries to put up as little money as possible, while the investor often puts up the full amount. People have the capital to speculate, but not invest, yet they go into situations as if they have the capital to invest. (For more ideas on this, see the discussion of scalpers, day traders, and long-term traders in Rule 35.)

How, then, do you learn to speculate when speculating is warranted and invest when investing is warranted? Aside from spending five years figuring out intuitively what market conditions warrant what trading approach, the only solution is to have two separate accounts—one for speculation, another for investments. This solution was presented to me by David Goldberg, a long-time member of the Chicago Board of Trade.

I had talked to David years ago about my inability to hang on to my winners and cut my losses short. I had been trading IBM stock and IBM options in the same trading account. After I sold out my IBM stock at slight profits I saw the stock go to new highs. The amount of money I left on the table was so great that I felt awful. Then, when I had IBM stock trades that were initial losers, I wouldn't get rid of them.

David suggested that I open two accounts—one for speculation and one for investments. He also told me that I should have bought IBM stock, which I wanted to hang on to for a long-term play in the investment account, and traded IBM stock from the speculation account for a short-term play. I thought it was foolish to have two accounts to trade just one stock because I was fixated on the redundant mechanics of creating two accounts. He, however, was making a very subtle point about the psychology and attitude a trader has toward a stock.

With two separate accounts, the long-term trade of IBM stock would have warranted a long-term outlook. If the stock dipped a quarter point from where I purchased it, I wouldn't panic. If it rallied a quarter point, I wouldn't be itching to take profits. If it dropped five points I wouldn't worry about it because it was a long-term trade. If it showed a five-point profit I still wouldn't unload, but would patiently wait for another five-point profit.

The speculation account would accommodate short-term trading strategies. If the same company's stock, IBM, was placed in the short-term account, I would panic if it dipped a quarter point and would try to unload it. If it rallied a quarter point, I would look to take profits immediately. I would never allow a five-point profit or loss to accumulate in the stock.

In this manner I would know exactly what is expected of me in managing each trading account. If the same stock was not doing what I designed the strategy to do in that account, I would liquidate that position. A side benefit is that I would not be able to rationalize my losses so easily, which is a problem with all unsuccessful traders.

There is no need to worry about profitable situations because you have defined each account, and each account performs to expectations. Getting profitable situations from each at the same time with the same stock is a godsend, but not in the game plan.

RULE 42

Don't Try to Predetermine
Your Profits

When I was a customer's man years ago, I always was asked one question to which I never knew the answer. If I saw a profitable play in the market, I would tell my clients about it. After I disclosed the fundamental and technical reasons why a particular market should be bought or sold, clients always asked how high or low I thought the market would go. They wanted my projections.

Naively, I would make some half-hearted guesses of where I expected the markets to go. Often, the market would get there and go beyond those initial projections.After having seen too many of these scenarios played out I modified my off the cuff projections by adding the phrase, " . . . at least," to my projections. Now, I won't even bother with coming up with projected numbers. When asked where the market is headed, I just say, "If it's a bull market, you've got to be long; if it's a bear market, you've got to be short."

I was caught off guard recently when Ben Larson, the host of Chicago's longest running television program on the stock markets, asked me to project the next day's market action. Trading for my own account over these many years has conditioned me to not talk about the markets to anyone, let alone his viewing audience. I blurted out, "Well, Ben, it looks like we might be up ten points tomorrow." Had I ended the interview with that statement, I would have looked brilliant because the market did go up 9.86 points the next day. Instead, I negated it by saying,

"Maybe we will even be down ten points." A colleague who saw the interview later mentioned that I sounded like an idiot, and I agreed. In reality, I couldn't have cared less where the market was headed the next day. I was bullish and I was long. That was all that mattered to me.

Consider the market as composed of two types of actions: a meandering type of action where prices don't move much, and a trending type of action where prices move violently.

When you initiate a trade, you buy a market at a fixed price. Your analysis shows that the price you bought is a good price area. You are acting on the here and now, and you want the market to appreciate in value. When the market starts to go up you don't have any idea where it will stop. You might have a projection of some price top, but you don't really know. The only way you will know is when the price actually makes a top and starts to head down. As much as we try to use all our technical tools we really do not know what future events will be, especially price action.

Limited by our inability to forecast precisely what prices will be in the future, we do what we consider the next best thing: We initiate positions based on the premise that a trend in motion stays in motion. We know this premise is credible because of our own observations of price charts. Prices move up and they move down. However, we must not conclude that a trend in motion will stop at a future price that is arbitrarily determined with present tense information. This is a flaw of many unsuccessful traders who have initiated long positions. Once their price objectives are reached, they unload their positions, only to see the market continue past their selling points. *Again, there is absolutely no reason why prices will stop at the points you predetermine.*

If the price of whatever you are long has enough fundamental and technical reasons to move higher, eventually past your initial entry point, you must know that the conditions affecting that market have changed to accommodate new information (in most cases, information that you did not predict). If you cannot forecast in advance what this new information is, what makes you think that you can forecast some price objectives that the market

190

has yet to reach? If you try to preordain where the market you are long will end, you will limit your potential profits.

For example, if you had gone long an S&P 500 index futures contract at 310 because it looked both fundamentally and technically bullish, you would have acted correctly on half the trade. The other half, that of allowing market action to cause the price of your holding to appreciate in value, must be played correctly. If you want to be a winning trader, you cannot send in limit orders to sell at some higher price before knowing the actual conditions affecting that market.

> *One of the best ways I know of to move with the flow of the market is to use stop loss orders that trail market action.*

When you place an order to buy, you expect the price to move up after your purchase. Why else would you buy? (Strangely enough, there are those masochistic traders who buy fully expecting the markets to go down afterwards. Their problems go deeper than the solutions this book can provide.) In a similar manner, when you place an order to sell, you expect the price to move down after your sale. Again, why else would you sell? The fact that you have created an order to sell at a higher price in your mind when you go long means that you are not allowing the market to tell you what it wants to do. Instead, you are dictating to the market what you want it to do by telling it at what level you want it to stop moving up.

One of the best ways I know of to move with the flow of the market is to use stop loss orders that trail market action. In the case where you enter an order to sell at a predetermined level of profits, your action is active in the markets. In the case where you follow the market up with trailing stop sell orders to protect your profits, your action is passive. When you are passive, you allow the market to tell you when it wants you to get out.

RULE 43

THE HUMAN SIDE OF EVERY PERSON IS THE GREATEST ENEMY TO SUCCESSFUL TRADING

Market professionals have always said that the inability to control the human element is the folly of the best traders. Throughout history we have seen the great speculators like Jesse Livermore and Arthur Cutten fall by the wayside when their trading approaches were misapplied to changing market conditions. Recently great speculators like Richard Dennis have failed when they applied once-applicable trading approaches to new market conditions.

It is an axiom in market folklore that the market will do whatever it has to do, to do the most damage to the most people. And the markets are situated extremely well to do this.

We humans, however, are frail. We can eat in only one way—through our mouths. We see in only one manner—when we open our eyes. We can feel and smell in only limited ways—when we touch with our skin and inhale through our noses. Yet we persist, foolishly at times, in regarding the markets to be as frail and as singular as we are. Some of us think that the markets are always in a trading range, so we always use trading market analytical techniques. Others contend that markets are always trending and, therefore, use trending market techniques all the time. Still others believe that markets are purely random and no single analytical approach is useful. The folly of humans is that some of us continue to use tools that are no longer applicable with new conditions. We assume that, once the markets are in any particular stage of activity, they will remain in that state.

> **Work on your personality to be flexible enough to change when change is warranted.**

There are times when successful trading or investing demands that a particular trading technique be used. There are other times when no *one* technique will work. Work on your personality to be flexible enough to change when change is warranted.

There is a time for everything, even in the markets. If there is inflexibility on the part of the trader there is failure.

Compounding the problems confronting inflexible traders is another problem inherent in the trading profession itself—stress. A Gallup poll conducted for the *Wall Street Journal* in August 1987 (reported in the September 29, 1987 edition), found that the job with the highest stress rating was commodity trading. Seventy-four percent of executives surveyed stated that trading involved the most stress, followed by advertising (42 percent), investment banking (21 percent), high technology (15 percent), legal profession (7 percent), and insurance (6 percent).

To alleviate this stress, traders often try the wrong solutions: they drink, they smoke, they do drugs. The successful trader deals with stress by picking and choosing the markets and conditions that he or she will trade in, virtually guaranteeing success.

But most people won't deal with trading stress in this manner because they have ingrained reasons to justify their successes elsewhere. To win in their own business, they must lose at trading. To feel good about making money quick and fast in the markets, they must work harder at their jobs. This is the wrong conditioning to the right responses.

As humans, we find varied ways to sabotage our successes in the markets. Some find the markets to be a very efficient way to sublimate seething emotions. If a trader argues at home, he won't let a trade get the best of him. He'll lose his shirt rather than have a market loser force him to do something he doesn't want to do. There's no way the trade is going to get the best of him, especially after his wife was so wrong.

As humans, we are not sure of ourselves. We rely on the experts in the trading business to guide us. Some of us even want experts to take over the management. Brokers are asked to do more trading for clients because the client is too busy to manage the money. These are the wrong reasons to trade. *You must trade because you want to make money.*

If you are unsuccessful at trading, stop for a moment and think about the real reasons you want to trade. Do you want to escape a boring job? Do you want to impress your friends? Such reasons are not strong enough to sustain traders while they learn the difficult business of trading. Make sure that you are trading to make money, and not because you want escapes.

Lack of confidence is a detriment to successful trading. Most unsuccessful traders don't have the nerves to pull the trigger. They take reckless shots in the markets and lose money. This, instead of abetting their confidence, reinforces their lack of it. If they were so good, why did they lose money?

You cannot do anything about the past; yet you can recognize the problems that being human poses for you as a successful trader. If you run into a string of losses, stop trading for a while. Take a break and come back again with all those problems resolved or held in abeyance.

RULE 44

BAN WISHFUL THINKING IN
THE MARKETS

The market acts on logic—its own logic. To be a successful trader, you must think like the market thinks and act like the market acts. This is the beginning of a regimen of appropriate actions that includes money, capital risk, and position management. Unsuccessful traders are those who feel that the markets must think and act like the traders do. Wishful thinking is one of many unsuccessful trading habits.

The enigma of market action is that at one stroke it encompasses reality, where market losses are immediate and brutal, and fantasy, where prices can be driven up or down beyond all expectations. Wishful thinking, uncoupled with a healthy perception of reality, is the application of fantasy to market actions.

Vic Rydberg was a trader at one of Chicago's futures exchanges and a very capable money manager. Before becoming a trader, he had been a professional thoroughbred handicapper. After graduating from college in the 1930s, he worked one year as an engineer. He found handicapping horses more interesting and embarked on a successful career playing the ponies "all the way from Florida to California." The ability that he developed to manage his risk capital while betting on horses made him an extremely successful handicapper. Unfortunately, this ability precluded him from being successful as a futures trader.

In retrospect I can see that because he was so successful in position management when he bet on the ponies he failed to learn the other important aspects of the markets when he tried to trade successfully. His risk management skills allowed Vic to stay in the trading game. He was successful in the sense that he survived, but unsuccessful in the sense that he made no real money. He was halfway to becoming a very successful trader.

> *Wishful thinking, uncoupled with a healthy perception of reality, is the application of fantasy to market actions.*

This chapter is not about his success in risk management and his ability to stay in a game which he hardly knew anything about, but about the ramifications of his ability to manage risk successfully. He was very prone to wishful thinking. He had a tendency to rationalize market actions that did not unfold according to his scenarios, and his trading profits suffered as a consequence of this.

Vic showed a disregard for market realities one day in his corn positions. The floor had expected an extremely bullish supply report for the existing corn crop. Vic had positioned well ahead of the report and bought a few contracts. He had no idea where he should liquidate his position if the market reacted badly to the bullish reports. All professionals must have an idea of where they get out if they are wrong.

The report came in extremely bullish, far more than anybody on the floor had expected. The market had closed for the day, so the next morning's expectations were that corn would open much higher, wheat higher, and soybeans higher to unchanged. Wheat opened higher and soybeans opened higher to unchanged, both according to floor traders' expectations. Corn, however, opened unchanged. It did not open lower, which would have been extremely bullish, and it did not open higher, which would have been according to expectations.

Most market players act more on fears and expectations than they do on reality. Had corn opened up, market action would have confirmed their expectations and they would have continued to move the prices up by buying more for themselves or getting others to buy. Because corn opened unchanged and failed to go up from the opening, the players had their worst fears confirmed.

As it turns out, corn prices dropped severely and touched limit down. They bounced up off limit, and then they traded down again. First the May option touched limit. Then the July option touched limit. Then September, then December. Finally, all one could see from the quote boards on the walls of the exchange was that everything was down the limit for the day. Then a pool of sell orders started to come in. First, it was 5,000 contracts offered limit down on the May option. Then a few hundred were offered in the new crop, December. By the end of the day, several million bushels of corn were offered in July, the end of the old crop. All across the board, millions of bushels of corn were offered for sale at limit down prices.

As soon as prices in the new crop corn overcame the sell orders by rallying from limit down, the sell orders cascaded into the front months. As corn prices remained limit down, the selling started to go into the wheat pit. First, they knocked the prices off the high for wheat. On the opening, wheat had rallied to intraday highs. Traders who were long corn had to sell something to hedge their losing positions outside of the corn pit because nobody wanted to buy corn. Some picked wheat to sell. Others picked oats. Still others picked soyabeans.

Vic was in the pit that morning with the rest of the traders trying to make sense of the market action. His perception of the market was turning into wishful thinking. I observed several stages in this process as the day wore on.

The first stage was denial of market action. Vic had expected the market to go up after the report. He had not planned on exiting his trades, except with profits, so he held onto his positions. Prices, however, continued to erode.

The second stage was the reinforcement of his initial decision to buy because it's bullish. Vic and other traders crowded around the Reuters broad tape machine to check the government reports. They all concurred that the reports were bullish and that being long was the right thing to do. Even in the late afternoon, they were hopeful that buying would come in and show them they were right. They consulted other demand reports and began reading between the lines: Russia would buy because it still had to fulfill a portion of its commitment for the year; China would buy because it was facing a severe drought; and India would buy because the monsoons has flooded the croplands. Prices, however, fell further.

The third stage crept in slowly. At this point they thought wishfully, hoped against reality, prayed for the miracle. As the market, several cents away from limit down, lulled observers to sleep and agitated long-sided traders, the fear that possibly no buy orders would come in germinated in one section of the trading pit. Before long, it became pervasive. One by one, the traders yawned in the pit, looked at their trading cards, and tallied their longs. They turned around and held their hands outwards. One offered 50 corn contracts, another offered 10. As traders started to unload, prices gave way and the market slid down like a hot knife through butter. Vic was able to unload his position on the next day's opening, which was several cents from limit down.

Vic buttonholed me shortly afterwards to talk about what had happened. All his sentences began with "It's bullish because . . . " and ended with " . . . I can't figure it out."

Wishful thinking now preempted rational thought.

Markets don't behave as you wish, but as they please. Markets have their own logic, and you must be able to discern what they are trying to tell you. The first consideration is: Is your trading equity appreciating or eroding? If the market does not conform to your game plan, you cannot stay with a position that is eroding your equity. That's wishful thinking. The equity you are losing is the market's way of telling you that, for whatever reasons, your market analysis was wrong. Take your loss and figure it out later.

RULE 45

BIG MOVEMENTS TAKE TIME TO DEVELOP

In the discussion of Rule 19, I talked about how important it is to use patience if you want to make substantial profits in the markets. The onset of options trading has caused some traders to move away from this philosophy of successful trading.

Trading history was made in 1973, when the Chicago Board Options Exchange, an offshoot of the Chicago Board of Trade, began trading listed stock options with standardized contracts. Until then, there were only two ways to make money in the stock markets: playing the right side of long-term trends to make capital gains and making above-average returns on dividends. The futures markets only have capital gains play. (However, in a sophisticated play with cost-of-carry markets, spreaders can make money on interest rates by buying the front end and selling the back end of an intramarket spread. The spreader takes delivery of the front end and holds it to deliver on the short side of the spread when it is due. The difference between the actual cost of carrying the futures contract and the delivered price of the short side of the spread is the profit. This play is difficult for the small speculator to implement because the margins of profits are razor thin.) All markets have capital gains plays, but only the capital markets have the interest coupons or dividends returns, the cost-of-carry play.

Before options came on the investment scene, there were no profitable ways to make money in markets that were trendless or had no sustained trending moves. When trends did occur, they unfolded over several years in the case of stocks and bonds, and several months in the case of futures. Options could be used to make money in *all* markets. In violently upward markets, speculators could make money by buying calls or selling puts. In down markets, puts could be bought or calls could be sold. In trendless markets, both calls and puts could be sold. In this manner, the speculator could now make money in sideways markets.

For the first time in market history, speculators could efficiently make money in markets that did not move. Sideways movements more often lead to up markets than to down markets. The traditional speculators waited for the up moves to begin so that they could latch onto the potential capital gains. Sideways markets did not move enough so that speculators could make any profits. However, they could make money with options by watching the markets erode the call and put premiums.

With the advent of options and the high profile of the trading range markets, the trader's skills in analyzing when a bull market or a bear market began or ended were no longer needed to make money on capital gains plays. Now, inexperienced younger traders who had no concept of how a bull or a bear market behaved could just sell put and call premiums. As the options eroded, the young traders' trading equity increased. For once, there was no need for new traders to accumulate market experience. As an options trader, all you had to do was to arbitrage differences in prices and sell premiums.

Options changed the behavior of the underlying market. The action of the stock market, where equity options took hold the earliest, illustrates the point I'm trying to make. The years from the beginning of 1986 to the end of 1988 saw three distinct market moves.

The first move saw the Dow Jones industrial averages climb from around the 1,900 level to the 2,700 level in less than one year. This historic surge was partially fueled by the options traders.

Then followed the quickest drop in history: The industrial averages lost one-third of their valuation in a two-month period, again fueled by options traders who called their strategy "portfolio insurance." The fact that the options players got bloodied the most in this market underscores the fact that the excesses caused by the use of options had to be compensated for by the violence of a one-day, 508-point drop. The outright short sellers—not the options players—made a bundle of money.

The stock market then staged one of the longest trading range markets after the sharpest drop. Again this was of historical significance, and again the premium sellers were actively making money. Markets such as these would not have existed before the options markets took hold. In making it easier for new traders to make money in the markets by selling premiums, we lost the need for analyzing market conditions.

> *There is no free lunch in this business. Successful traders make money in long, drawn out bull markets. These are markets that take time to develop.*

The cycle has made one complete revolution and we are now back at the beginning of all market strategies: Determine the trend of the market to make the most money. The young traders who have made big money in options will be forced to fall back on traditional ways of analyzing market movements if they want to take advantage of capital gains plays.

There is no free lunch in this business. Successful traders make money in long, drawn out bull markets. These are markets that take time to develop.

RULE 46

LOOK FOR REASONABLE PROFITS

We've all heard stories about people making a lot of money in the markets. Perhaps you know someone who bought Time stock just before the buyout, in which it shot up $47 in one day, or someone who bought soybeans just before the drought. The beans moved from $5.50 a bushel to more than $10 a bushel. That's about a $21,000 move on one contract in two months. These events don't occur often, but when these events do occur and are reported in the media, the public is led to believe that making 100 percent a year or more on one's capital is the norm.

I have made an average 50 percent net return on my own investments and speculations without opening margin and haircut accounts. This includes all the years in which I broke even or lost money in the markets because I was learning about the business and all the years in which I broke even or lost money in the markets because I was an expert.

I started trading with about $5,000 in my account. During the first year I scalped like crazy and made about a $30,000 profit at the end of the year. I made about a 600 percent return on my original capital. Of course, being young and inexperienced, I spent all of my profits. At the start of the second year, I wondered how much return I could get for the amount of capital I was using. Would it be 600 percent again, or could I double it to maybe 1,200 percent? At the end of the second year I again turned my $5,000 start capital to $30,000 of profits. Again I worked like a madman on the floor. And not knowing that even rainbows end somewhere, I spent like a madman. At the start of the third year I had $5,000 in the account and wondered whether this would be the year in which I would double my profits. Of course, the question that I should have asked was how was I able to get two 600 percent return years in a row! As it evolved, the third year turned into a disaster.

> *I have made an average 50 percent net return on my own investments and speculations without opening margin and haircut accounts. This includes all the years in which I broke even or lost money in the markets as a learner or later as an expert.*

Out of this experience I developed my own little rule of business management: I figured out that the harder I worked my money, the faster it went about finding other owners.

I know that if you spend time to learn about the markets and then trade and invest in them, you must get a better than average rate of return. The average rate of return is what the professionals pay you after they make their profits and overhead! This pays for your professional involvement in the markets.

However, once in a while there are stellar moves in the marketplace that will make a pauper a prince. Professionals, because they are full-time players in the markets, have opportunities to latch onto such stellar moves once in a while. What most people don't understand is that in order to take advantage of such moves, they must have enough capital in their accounts to handle larger than normal positions. They must also have resources to research their investments or speculations and support people on the floor to handle the execution of their trades. In other words, they must have an infrastructure of support that will allow them to capitalize on these plays. Most traders don't. They cannot jump from trading 10 contracts or 1,000 shares of stock to 100 contracts or 10,000 shares overnight.

Since most traders don't have the infrastructure already in place, they cannot take full advantage of the moves without risking their livelihood. If they can make better than average returns without stepping out of their normal trading environment, they will survive to capitalize on the next stellar move. And let me assure you that if you miss this one move, others will soon come along.

A colleague told me about an equity options trader who made $128,000 on $58,000 of trading capital in four months. This was about a 220 percent return on his capital, nonannualized. In the height of public participation in the options markets, profits were much higher because the markets were younger and less efficient.

What is not known about performances such as these is the actual net return. Under more discreet questioning I discovered that because of the margining of his positions, this trader was borrowing about $490,000 to cover his positions. His haircut was about $575,000. Through the magic of exchange and industry regulations, the trader increased his trading power by tenfold.

Then the expenses started to erode his profits. First there was the $5,000 a month overhead he had to pay to get computer equipment, data services, and clerical help. The trader paid himself no salary and worked strictly for profits. Then there were commission costs. As an exchange member, his commissions were as low as 30¢ a contract, yet they still amounted to $15,000 a month. His total overhead was about $20,000 a month.

For four months of activity, his total expenses amounted to about $80,000. Deducting this from his profits of $128,000, he netted about a $48,000 return every trimester. His annualized net profits would be about three times the $48,000, or $144,000. His weekly net profits were about $3,000. If he were to make $144,000 net profit every year and his commission costs amounted to $15,000 a month at 30¢ a contract (that comes out to 50,000 contracts traded every month), he would be making about 24¢ profit on each trade.

In a week of frenzied stock takeover activity, this trader lost $15,000. He had to close out his options positions in takeover stocks at big losses. One week of losses offset five weeks of profits.

Still, if you look at the amount of net profits at the end of the year, $144,000, and see what capital he had to do this with,

$58,000, you would see that he was still making about a 248 per-
cent net return a year. To get this return he had to take
advantage of exchange membership and extremely beneficial
margining and haircut regulations. If he had to come up with
the full amount of haircut money, $575,000, to make $144,000 a
year, his annual rate of return would fall to 25 percent a year.

A 25 percent annual rate of return is sustainable. A 248 percent rate of return is not sustainable on a long-term basis. The
fact that the trader has beneficial capital requirements is balanced by the fact he is subject to volatile losses when the
leveraging worked against him. Since he is a professional, he
must know how to control his losses so that he can capitalize on
his advantages.

If you want to trade the markets and make profits over the
long term, you must not expect to sustain extremely high rates
of return. In fact, you must be leery of situations that offer high
rates over a short period, for they also carry an above-average
risk of losing all your trading capital.

RULE 47

FOOLS CAN TAKE PROFITS, BUT WISE TRADERS KNOW WHEN TO TAKE A LOSS

Let's discuss why we emotionally cannot take a loss when all practical considerations point out that we should and must.

When we close out open trades that are profitable we feel very good. We know that the profits will be translated into benefits for ourselves. It's the reason why we strive to trade the markets. We want to make money from them.

We can get into trading positions which result in no profits and no gains. Hence, we trade and trade and realize that we aren't making any profits, nor accruing any losses. We dismiss this experience as ongoing learning and hope that as time progresses we will not waste any more time on taking on positions which don't make us money. These trading positions make no money for us, but they don't do what losing positions do to us.

However, the other side of the trading equation is that more often than not our trading positions result in losses. These losses always start out as open trade losses and only when we close them out do they then become permanent losses. The losses do not create warm feelings because they prevent us from making money and instead cause us to lose money. We now don't even make money: we lose our money. This happens when we don't trade well.

One of the ironies of trading is that most of us do not talk about our losses. We talk about our winnings with vigor, how-

> *The act of taking a loss when your judgment is wrong is market wisdom in action.*

ever. We hide our losses; we are ashamed of them as signs of our failures. People perceive our judgment as defective when they know that we have sustained losses. This explains why I never talk about either my losses or winnings. Because I don't talk about anything I do in the markets, I face no embarrassment, nor do I have victories to regale. This is my attempt at trying to maintain a balanced perspective on being able to control losing situations professionally.

I have become my own self-sustained trader. Just as you should be striving for this. Until the time comes when you are tight-lipped about your trading prowess and weakness you will need to talk both about your winners and losers to others. It's natural for us to communicate our desires and ambitions to others when we are in the process of formulating them; it's a form of goal formation. We create goals of attaining success and diminishing failure by verbalizing our desires and ambitions. The more we can create an environment which supports our pursuit of these goals the more successful we can become.

My advice is never to talk about your winners or losers. But you might say that if you never talk about your winners or losers, especially losers, you will never find the solutions to eliminate the losers.

This is a valid objection. If someone other than me can prove to me that they have a better approach to the markets than I have, then let them give me enough information to whet my interest. Once intrigued, I will pursue the knowledge. I don't think they can. And this is the exact approach you should take toward all these newfangled ideas and techniques to better and more consistent profits.

Have I taken the path that I caution you not to take? Yes, I have. I believed once that what others taught or professed to know was more than what I knew. For a period in my early development as a trader, I followed up on all the talk and advertisements of products and services claiming that they would reveal their secrets if I merely paid several hundred dollars. At the beginning the knowledge I acquired was beneficial since my knowledge of the markets was limited, but as I learned more and more I realized that the people knew less and less. I became more leery of buying these products and services. After I discovered that what most of these people considered to be secret I actually already knew but applied somewhat differently, I concluded that these purveyors didn't know any more than I did. Still, I paid to learn that basic fact.

What does my experience of learning that the experts didn't know more than me have anything to do with you being a wise man to take losses? I became a wiser trader after I realized that I already knew what these people thought they knew when it came to market knowledge.

I paid to find out that they knew less than me. This was very critical in my self-discovery process. After I realized that these experts who were successfully managing money or writing best-selling market books or consulting with huge financial institutions didn't know more than me, I concluded that whatever I was seeking to know, it was not necessary in order for me to be as successful as these people were! This was the revelation to me. But, until I went through this actual process I couldn't come to the conclusion that I already had all the knowledge for successfully trading the markets!

The only missing element was being able to put all the bits and pieces of knowledge into one cohesive plan of huge success. This missing element struck me one day in a brief flash of insight.

The act of taking a loss when your judgment is wrong is market wisdom in action. By itself this act is negligible in impact, but in the context of a trading career, this singular act is highly symbolic of your success as a trader.

The act of taking losses when your judgment is wrong implies many things about the person who is trading. Some of these are:

1. You are humble enough to admit defeat in face of market-dictated reality. Your positions turn into losers regardless of how well you've analyzed them. The fact that you get rid of them implies your admission that the markets are bigger than you, which they are.

2. You view the markets as ongoing and that you can come back tomorrow, the next day, or even a year from now and still trade successfully. You know that you can always get back into the markets because you've accepted the fact that your current losing trade must be closed out because it is not behaving according to your forecasts. This gives an element of faith that what will be will be.

3. Taking care of losses first is the key to market participation longevity. Fight and run away, to trade another day.

4. You understand that taking losses is not an element of taking profits. Taking losses is only used to manage your losses, not make money. The act of taking a profit is a profit-taking action, and not the act of preventing a loss. You are wise enough to know that the act of taking a loss is not a profit-making action, but a way to prevent further loss. The profit-taking action adds to your equity, but the loss-prevention action doesn't add to anything.

5. You've wised up to the real game of trading.

Learning to take losses is not as simple as just telling your broker to get rid of the bad trades in the marketplace. To get to the point of taking losses as a matter of fact requires a depth of understanding of market action. Once you've realized that developing the ability to take losses when you are wrong is the first critical step to your market success you are indeed a wiser trader.

RULE 48

IF YOU CAN'T MAKE MONEY TRADING THE LEADING ISSUES, YOU AREN'T GOING TO MAKE IT TRADING THE OVERALL MARKETS

The original intention of this rule was to show that the leading issues led the rest of the markets. If you were notable to read the tape activity of the leading issues, and hence forecast their future movements, you would not be able to read what the rest of the market was doing.

The market moves in waves of buying and selling activity. The rule discussed in this chapter was conceived when the overall markets were traded as individual issues. As long as market players were only able to trade individual issues, if they had an opinion about the whole market the genie was contained in the bottle. Once the exchanges opened trading in indices and at margins that were even less than individual stock margins prior to the 1929 crash, a completely different set of market interpretations had to be created.

To understand how the market operates in waves of buying and selling activities, it is necessary to see how its various components interact with one another.

The stock market can be broken into three basic tiers or activity groups: the primary, the secondary, and the tertiary. These groups can be divided according to institutional interest, trading volume, and investment grades. For a quick and easy way of segregating these stocks into viable groups for analysis, just look at their prices. The primaries are the highest priced, the secondaries are the second highest, and the tertiaries are the cheapest to own.

> *The primaries are the highest priced, the secondaries are the second highest, and the tertiaries are the cheapest to own.*

In the primary group we can see IBM, Digital Equipment, Procter & Gamble, General Motors, Ford Motors, Time, Inc., and other companies that are the backbone of the United States economy. They are the blue chips.

The secondary group comprises companies like Warner Communications, Paramount, USX Corporation, Syntex, Exxon, General Electric, American Express, and Motorola. The quality of these stocks is high and, depending on the fundamentals of these companies, they are sometimes found in the primary group. Texaco was once considered a bluechip issue but is now classified as a secondary stock.

The tertiary group is made up of stocks that range from dogs to fallen blue chips like Navistar (formerly known as International Harvester) and Mansville (formerly known as Johns Mansville).

This categorization of the stock market is critical to being able to read market activity correctly. Overall market activity can be seen as buying and selling interests by market participants. Their overall buying and selling will be revealed in the strength and weakness of the three groups.

The bottom of a bear market is distinguished from the beginning of a bull market by activity in the primary groups of stocks. After all three groups of stocks have found bottoms at the end of a bear market, buying interests will first appear in the primary group. The big players like insurance companies, mutual funds, and heavily capitalized individuals will start to nibble at the fallen blue chips. Stocks that once traded at $100 and now are trading at $30 or $40 will be bought quietly. Technical indicators will show accumulation of these blue chips.

After a severe bear market, the uninformed investors will have no capital to accumulate stocks for long-term investments. Meanwhile, because the blue chips are the strongest companies financially, they can weather bear market fundamentals that have permeated the whole economy. The weaker companies have gone bankrupt, leaving the blue chips, by default, thriving on reduced market shares. The informed investors and companies know that the blue chips will survive.

In the process of buying the blue chips, the big players start to move up the prices. Supply decreases while demand increases. As prices of the blue chips move from the $30 to $40 range to the $60 to $70 range, the economy starts to improve. While this is happening, companies start to rehire the employees that they laid off during the bear market. As the workers replenish their investment coffers with money, they start to look at investable securities. The primaries have gone to recent highs and have moved out of the purchasing range of these recently enriched workers. The interest is now to look for value in secondary issues.

As the buying action moves to the secondaries, they climb from the $20 to $30 range to the $40 to $50 range. Meanwhile, the primaries continue to show strength either because of rotation activity, where prices are locked in a trading range, or because certain primary issues manage to double and quadruple in price due to particular situations that reflect heightened interest in whatever game Wall Street is playing at the time: In the 1960s it was conglomerates; in the 1980s it was mergers and acquisitions.

The moneyed investors rotate their interests in the primaries and create opportunities that will help them unload their much-appreciated holdings to other buyers.

Under the strength of leading issues they will unload the weaker sisters. Under the strength of IBM, other computer stocks like Texas Instruments and Digital Equipment will find more buyers.

As the primaries are rotated and the secondaries are accumulated and marked up, poorly capitalized investors start to wend their way into investment traps by looking at the tertiaries. Industry insiders have always regarded interests in the tertiary issues as a harbinger that the bull market is about over. As some market players look to value tertiary issues considerably above what fundamentals would justify, informed investors might even start to put out shorts in the secondary groups. The primary issues were the first to go up and they will be the last to go down.

As the unloading of the appreciated holdings continues, pockets of weakness appear in the leading issues. Once in a while a primary issue might drop several points for no apparent reason, while the rest of the market continues unchanged. This is one of the first signs that distribution is about over and a campaign to drive stocks down is about to begin.

Bear markets in stocks begin while the economy is still in a bull market. Under cover of darkness the enemy creeps in. The cycle then resumes. Bear markets cannot begin until informed investors have had a chance to unload their holdings. The collapse of the stock market in October 1987 was so fast that insiders were not able to unload their holdings. Since the bulk of the holders of the stocks at 2,750 on the Dow Jones industrials were also the holders of these stocks with the averages at 1,650, it was easier for them to buy more stock than to sell what they already owned.

The most popular technical analysis technique within the last 50 years has been the revival of the Elliott Wave theory developed by Ralph Nelson Elliott and popularized by Robert Prechter under the initial instructions of A. J.Frost. The Elliott Wave theory was originally conceived as a way to discern wave formations in the Dow Jones industrial averages. The patterns that unfolded could be used to interpret overall market activity. Some individual traders and analysts have been able to use the theory to discern similar patterns in individual stock issues and futures contracts.

Since the overall market could be forecasted with relative success, it was initially easy for wave followers to trade individual stock issues well. However, as early as 1984 I noticed that the Dow Jones industrials waves that formed from 1975 on did not follow previous formation creations. The corrections were becoming lengthier, and the impulse waves were becoming more violent.

213

The increasing polarity of violent impulse waves from lengthier corrective waves was accelerated by the fact that in 1984 Robert Prechter traded stock index options using the Elliott Wave theory with great success. His accomplishment was hailed throughout the investment world. There had been some interest in trading the indices with the Elliott Wave theory, but it was Prechter's phenomenal trading of index options that brought this trading approach into the light.

For once we witnessed a phenomenon the investment world had never seen before: Market interests that had been forced in the past to be played out in individual stock issues could now be played out in actual trading in the indices. Not only could it be played out in such a manner, it also could be traded with great success with a technique that worked very well: the application of the Elliott Wave theory.

As in all market trading strategies that eventually die because of their own successes, the same advantage that Elliott Wave theorists had over others when trading the Dow Jones industrial averages invalidated the Elliott Wave theory. As long as others could not trade the indices using the Elliott Wave theory, it remained valid in forecasting wave movements. Once the indices could be traded using the theory, it no longer worked.

RULE 49

LEADERS OF TODAY MAY NOT BE THE LEADERS OF TOMORROW

There are many ways to forecast future price movements, but the most basic way is to look at past price action and try to determine a pattern. If you can see a pattern that repeats with a greater than 50 percent probability, you will be able to forecast future price movements. This does not necessarily mean that you will make money, for that is a question of position management.

In looking for stocks that lead the rest of the market, you are basically looking for a pattern that repeats. The money is not made by trading the leading stock, but by trading the stocks that follow it.

When the leader starts its move, traders start to buy stocks that have followed this leader in the past. The trader makes money when the followers eventually go up in price. Within the group of followers there are clearly defined degrees of how fast and how often they follow the leader. Knowing which of the follower stocks are laggards is also important because when the laggards no longer follow the follower stocks, the strength of the leader stock is diminishing. It is time to cut back the commitment of capital to the followers.

The leader can be an individual stock or a group of stocks in the same industry. In the intermediate bull market of 1986, the leader was a group of technology stocks that included IBM, Texas Instruments, Digital Equipment, and Hewlett Packard.

These technology stocks were led by IBM. Once IBM found its intermediate target, it rotated nicely in a trading range while the other technology stocks followed it up. As soon as traders saw IBM move, they started picking up on the nontechnology stocks, and eventually the whole market went up.

> *In looking for stocks that lead the rest of the market, you are basically looking for a pattern that repeats.*

There is one problem with following the leader stock over time: The strength of the stock eventually flags, and other stocks take over as the leaders. One way to discern when the mantle of strength is being handed over to other issues is by observing how the laggard stocks behave. In normal markets, where the follower stocks move up after the lead stock makes new highs for the move, the laggard stocks also will follow to the upside in their own proportionate pricing. If the leader moves five points in a week, the laggards might only move two points. If the laggards retreat instead of move, the strength of the overall market is in question.

Another way to observe the weakness of the leader stock is to watch stocks that in the immediate past followed the leader upward. If the leader stock stops going up, watch what the immediate followers are doing. If immediate followers show strength and continue upward, you can conclude that market strength is being transferred to the followers. The current leader will soon become a follower.

Follower stocks also have rotational strength. The Digital Equipments and the Hewlett Packards of their respective industries will take over the lead when the leader falters. Because of the number of issues available in the markets today, it is best to define market strength by industry. Barron's and Standard & Poor's have created their own industry groups. By creating composite numbers for each industry group, traders can monitor the activity of one group relative to other groups.

The analysis of relative price movements can be used also with futures contracts—within futures contracts themselves (soybeans) and within a futures complex such as grains or metals.

In the first case, within futures contracts themselves, you can observe strengths or weaknesses among different expiration months in the same contract. For example, you can track and compare the relative price movements of each of the expiration months. This is watching the movement of spreads between two different months. This type of analysis is considerably easier than tracking the varied groups in the stock market because the demarcations of groupings in the stock market are more subjective and there are more details to learn about individual companies. In the futures market, if you decide to track the movements of the soybean contract you need only specialize in soybeans. You don't have to specialize in a different underlying futures.

Tracking groups of commodities is more interesting, and more difficult. To track the metals complex, for example, you will have to know about the price movements of the individual commodities such as silver, gold, palladium, and platinum, and how they relate to the others. Tracking the strength of silver can be informative if the price of gold does not follow silver, but the analysis has to be more detailed and in-depth. The volatility due to the low margin requirements makes the futures industry less forgiving of mistakes. If you acquire a position in a laggard stock that does not move up with the leader, you have ample time and opportunities to unload the position without damage to your equity. In the stock market, laggards cannot become leaders, because their price action is too sluggish. In the volatile futures markets, laggards can be leaders to the downside, so futures requires more study and intense monitoring of market activity.

Sympathetic movements in the futures markets exist, but rarely and only under conditions of great strength. Unless the market is a raging bull, the trader will find it difficult for all the commodities within that complex to move in concert.

Today's market leaders may not be the leaders tomorrow, so it would be foolish to trade the followers based on this "expected" action of current leaders in the future. If the leaders show signs of weakness, look at the immediate followers and see if the others will follow when they move upward. The weakness that develops in the laggards is the first signal that the current move up is about over.

RULE 50

IGNORE STATISTICAL REPORTS IN BEAR MARKETS

Play bear markets differently than bull markets when it comes to using statistical reports. It is generally accepted practice to disregard statistical reports on securities together with records of past earnings and dividends.

My self-training and experience has taught me that in bear markets, sell anything and everything. First sell out all longs, then sell short. Are there any exceptions, i.e., going long in bear markets? Yes, but to find the exceptions is similar to trying to find the proverbial needle in a haystack: it's possible, but not probable. Don't waste your efforts to find the needle; your time can be efficiently used to find the next weak stock to short. It will be lining up for you to pick out.

In the same manner that all stocks go up in a bull market, all stocks go down in a bear market. You will be exposing yourself to guaranteed losses by going long in bear markets.

If the public was enchanted with a stock during the late stages of the bull market cycle, you can expect the stock to drop more when the public becomes disenchanted with the stock's performance in the bear market. It's in the nature of market action. The heros of yesterday's bull market will be among the first to be rounded up and shot in the next bear market.

How do statistics and fundamentals enter into the analysis of these stocks? Very simply, they will turn out bad, again supporting reasons why the stocks must be sold or shorted.

The degree of bearishness of the markets can be inferred if a

> **By the time you get the numbers to justify the price action in this quarter, the price will have been eroded further!**

group of stocks in the same industry drops when bullish news appears for one of its members; the degrees of bearishness rotate from the weakest to the strongest stock in that industry, which is only logical. If you are a portfolio manager interested in personal computer stocks and all have been taking this to the downside because of the general bearishness of the markets, you will be looking for reasons to liquidate your holdings in the personal computer industry. If a bullish set of numbers comes out for one still bullish stock in that group, you will unload your other stocks in that group and concentrate your buying in that one bullish stock—pure Darwinism in action. The strong get stronger and the weak get weaker.

At best, the future numbers for most sectors will show weakness. You must get rid of all longs in bear markets because of fundamental reasons; these numbers will worsen as the bear market ensures. You must go short in bear markets because of timing techniques. Understand the distinction between ridding yourself of longs and going short; understand the use of fundamental numbers and technical techniques.

You must ignore all statistical numbers in bear markets and concentrate on market action instead because the numbers which are coming out at the present are *reflective of what happened, not what will be happening*. In general, all these statistical numbers reflect generally better numbers from the past than what will be shown later, which are results of the present and the immediate future.

In bear markets you don't have the same privileges that come with bull markets. In bull markets, you can delay your entry into a stock that is going up in price. You don't lose money, but you lose potential profits by getting involved in this lead of price versus lag of statistical numbers. In bear markets, you actually lose money if you buy because prices erode while you are holding the positions. By the time the real reasons come out, you will have lost substantial amounts of money.

219

The correct way to play bear markets is to sell in anticipation of weaker statistical numbers.

What good does it do you if last quarter's earnings were unchanged from the previous quarter's when the price action of the stock is reflecting bearishness by going down? By the time you get the numbers to justify the price action this quarter, the price will have been eroded further! Yes, you will eventually get the numbers which will justify the current pricing, but by then the pricing would have dropped as much as it could already. You will then be sitting with a large unrealized loss in your holdings.

Round numbers for stocks such as $50, $75, $100, etc., were markers in the past for these stocks on the way up. These same price levels will not hold as support and reversal areas in bear markets. On the way up they were areas of buying, on the way down they will be price areas of supply. Over the last several years I've noticed a perverse interest on the part of traders to purposefully try to push prices immediately past these numbers in either direction. It's sort of a challenge to them to see if they can crack these even numbers. In the past there were temporary reversals. Nowadays, I don't know whether or not the types of players in the markets are more sophisticated, but these levels appear as challenges to traders. These traders are intent on pushing past these even numbers, some even on the first try.

RULE 51

TRADE COUNTERTREND
WITH A PORTION OF YOUR
ORIGINAL COMMITMENT

According to an old trading rule, "When the market is in an up-trend and you wish to take advantage of a little shake-out to come, trade short, but only with 1/3 of the capital used on the long-side. If you usually purchase 300 shares on the upside, trade only 100 shares short. The reverse is true of a downtrend market."

I had not read anything that showed specifically how to vary your position risk to minimize equity loss in case your analysis is incorrect. Then I read this rule.

This rule specifically tells you how much you should risk on countertrend trades. Most of us have always presumed that we risk a portion of our total position commitment, not of our total equity, on trending trades, but we were never sure, or at least never aware, of how much to risk of our total commitment, if any, in countertrend trades. We presumed that if we traded 300 shares from the long side in bullish markets, we would also risk 300 shares in countertrend trades.

I had always dismissed trading against the trend anyway, so to take $\frac{1}{2}$, $\frac{1}{3}$, or any fraction of the amount I would normally risk on trend trades and put it up against the risks in countertrend trades had not occurred to me. I learned from the market's brute force that it didn't make sense for me to trade against the trend. I'm not that lucky that I can skirt damage by trading against the major market trend. At most, I would just sell out previously established longs at overbought conditions in bull markets.

In the past, when I needed some action, an "action-fix" so, to speak, and the markets were in a corrective phase, I would take a flyer on a few lots of futures or shares of stock. In the back of my mind I was always mindful to get out of those trades speedily if the market resumed its primary trend. Generally, taking flyers didn't make or lose a lot of money for me. Taking flyers merely served to appease my yet untempered need for action.

Let's use an example to see the problem with the rule in this chapter: The market is in a sustained bull move to the upside; any day now it's headed for a correction. You have established long positions of 9,000 shares of stock, or commodities, which you've picked up at cheaper prices. You have large unrealized capital gains. What do you do in this scenario?

Close to a presumed intermediate top you can perform any of the following three actions with your positions and take the results:

1. You can sell out all your longs, stay out of the market completely and look for other trade opportunities. The majority of new to intermediate traders do exactly this and wind up kicking themselves for missing a big portion of a bull market move.
2. You can sell out none of your longs and stay in the markets. Here you are really a long-term trader and will hold to your long positions come hell or high water. This type of investor makes money, but not as much as a trader-type who can deftly move correctly in and out of the markets to take advantage of the market's intermediate savings.
3. You can sell out part of your longs and stay out of the market until you see a better price opportunity to get back in.

The benefits of choosing one of these three options depend on which method will make you the most money. It's not a question of not ringing the cash register. You already have profitable positions, so it's merely a decision of taking them or not, and if taken, how much of the profits to realize.

The next set of options centers on what type of risk you should now take. Remember that if you choose one of these next four options, treat it as a separate trade from whatever choice you made on the first set of three options, regardless of whether your choice on the first set affects your choice of the second set of options.

> *Markets do not usually stop abruptly and head in the opposite direction overnight.*

Then you attempt to take advantage of a correction that's due to come by choosing one of the following four:

1. You can sell short 9,000 shares of stock after you've unloaded your longs in the above manner.
2. You can sell short $\frac{1}{3}$ of your long commitment, i.e., 3,000 shares after you've unloaded your longs in the above manner.
3. You can stay out of the market by not going short any commitment after you've unloaded your longs in the above manner.
4. You can sell more than your initial position of 9,000 shares, perhaps 12,000 shares, to take advantage of the ensuing correction.

From my own trading experience I would not sell short 9,000 or more shares of stock. I would elect not to short, and I would not also stay out of the market on the correction. I would sell short a partial commitment if I wanted a little market action.

I base my decisions on several reasons. First, the market has not shown me that the main uptrend has reversed. Markets do not usually stop abruptly and head in the opposite direction overnight. Unfortunately, most of us recall the few exceptions when the market has done this. However, markets need time to reverse directions. So until a bit of time has passed I would continue to buy the market. Until this happens, I refrain from shorting.

Second, if I were forced to try to go short I would not take on more positions than originally intended. If I had ridden the move to the upside with 9,000 shares, my profit on the 9,000 shares is there. Let's now figure out what happens when I decide to trade a larger number of shares at the supposed top of the market. I would now expose myself to an additional risk that I did not burden myself with on the way up. With a position of

9,000 shares, a $2.00 move up makes an $18,000 profit. With a position of 12,000 shares, to lose that $18,000 profit all the stock has do is to move against me by $1.50. The chance of a stock, regardless of market position, moving $1.50 in either direction in a day to day fluctuation is better than it moving $2.00.

Why put myself in a greater risk position for losses than the risk position to make the profits? Unfortunately, a majority of investors or traders do this. They trade a constant number of shares on the way to profits and then somewhere at the top they double up the number of shares traded, not necessarily going in the opposite direction of the previous trend, and get taken out of all profits with a normal market reversal. The markets have behaved as always; so have the unsuccessful traders who at the market tops placed all their accumulated profits at risk by increasing their position risk.

Now comes manipulating the market by shorting a number of shares smaller than the original commitment to make the profits. If you wanted to take advantage of the market's supposed down move, shorting a small position is better than sorting a large position. Still, shorting no position, while the market is still bullish, is better than shorting anything.

I can offer an alternative to the above four choices that has worked out well for me: While the markets are still bullish, instead of shorting the very stock that I am making bullish plays in, I would short another stock which is technically weaker. I would then be long a strong stock and short a weak stock, a spread between stocks of different strengths in a bull market.

Here again, depending on market stages and conditions, the stock I short in a still generally bullish market will often turn out to go neither up nor down. It acts as the dead leg of a spread.

Hedge funds essentially operate in this manner, however. This now leads us to the next rule on how you can use the market to absorb huge amounts of capital.

RULE 52

Trade the Active Stocks and Futures

One of the yardsticks I use to analyze market activity of a particular stock issue or futures contract is the volume. I prefer to trade issues that have consistent trading volume activity.

Professional money managers do not trade low volume issues with no liquidity, but they do put on long-term positions in these issues based on careful fundamental analysis. They are, in effect, buying a company to own it and become part of management. Berkshire Hathaway, a former textile manufacturer turned into an investment vehicle by Warren Buffet, started off by accumulating formidable interests in smaller, well-run companies. It was essentially the only player in these companies and could dictate how the stock was acquired and distributed. For trading purposes, these same money managers will go towards the more liquid issues.

In futures, the less active markets are havens for floor traders and dens of bad execution for public orders. If you have ever traded any illiquid issues, you will know that the skids on the price executions are horrible. After all, floor traders make a living on public order flow. Unless you have very good fundamental and bullish analysis of the thin markets, it is best not to trade them.

I prefer to trade in markets with quite a bit of volume activity because I can enter and exit positions with ease. Remember, when you buy a stock, you are adding to the demand for the stock, so the price will probably move up when you buy. On the other side of the coin, when you sell a stock, you are adding to supply, so the price will probably move down when you sell. In either case, you want the stock price to go up *after* you buy and down after you sell. You don't want the market to move away from you when you are actually executing the trade. In a broad, liquid market, prices are less likely to move away from you when you are executing the trade because of the huge amount of trading interests in that market. In illiquid markets, you can essentially *become* the market by buying or selling a few shares or contracts; in such cases you might possibly be chasing the market to execute your trade.

> *I prefer to trade in markets with quite a bit of volume activity because I can enter and exit positions with ease.*

I also stick with the active markets because they are less vulnerable to unfair manipulation. Note that I said "unfair" manipulation. As an experienced trader I assume that there is manipulation in all markets. When an experienced trader finds market manipulation going on, he or she wants to trade on the side of the big vested players. Substantial profits can be made riding the coattails of a properly marketed issue or futures. It only makes sense that investors or speculators with vested interests in a particular market would want to do whatever they can to support their positions: buying more to support, telling influential friends about the good investment, hyping future prospects of the investments—all legal activities. When the big players are supporting an issue or otherwise making their presence known to analysts, profits are easier to accumulate. Most big players will trade only in well-capitalized markets with broad participation. They don't want to get caught holding the bag if their analysis is incorrect. It doesn't take much to monopolize an inactive market; once that happens, other big players won't trade the issue because they know that the last one in the market will be the last one out. You, as a small trader or investor, don't want to get trampled when these big players start a run for the exit doors while you're walking in.

Information is readily available in widely traded issues. Thinly traded issues are quoted only in the pink sheets and have only a handful of market makers to provide information. Cocoa futures have so little trading activity that you have to obtain special reports to find out anything about it. With less information, you have less to come up with for an informed decision; you will be trading and speculating on incomplete information. I like to control where I send my trading capital.

Unsuccessful traders emphasize only the first part of a trade, the part that involves accumulating information to decide what to do in the markets, and ignore the last part of a trade, the part that involves getting out of a trade. Even if you were to get into a thinly traded issue and see it appreciate substantially in value, you can't realize the profit unless someone buys the issue from you. In illiquid issues, potential buyers are few and far between. You might think that there is always a buyer of any issue, whether you are selling your position out at a profit or at a loss; unfortunately, every other public investor in that thin issue is thinking along the same lines. When public investors start to run out the door at the same time, the bid–ask spread for the issue starts to widen and eventually disappears altogether. Market makers will make a market as long as they can profit from it; they will be the first ones to protect their trading positions when push comes to shove. In thoroughly liquid markets with depth of participation, there is always a buyer at a price that is not a giveaway.

If you are cashing in on a profitable position, you can afford to give away a few dollars to get a close out position. If you are cutting your losses, you want to try to sell at your entry price, but, failing that, you want to get as close as you can to the last price. It is difficult to cut your losses in illiquid markets.

Table 52.1 Trading Liquidity: Futures

(From Technical Analysis of Stocks and Commodities, June1989. Used with permission)

Commodity Futures	Exchange	% Margin	Effective % Margin	Contracts to Trade for Equal Dollar Profit	Relative Contract Liquidity
Eurodollar	IMM	0.4	7.4	5	 100
Standard & Poor's 500	CME	10.0	24.9	1	 62
US Treasury Bonds	CBT	2.8	14.7	4	 58
Crude Oil	NYM	10.0	19.4	6	....
Soybeans	CBT	4.2	7.7	3	......
Silver	CMX	8.6	9.2	2	......
Gold	CMX	5.2	17.5	5	.....
Japanese Yen ¥	IMM	1.8	5.00	2	.....
Sugar-World #11	CSCE	14.7	23.0	7	....
Corn	CBT	4.5	9.7	10	....
10-Year Treasury Notes	CBT	1.6	11.2	5	...
West German Mark DM	IMM	2.1	5.7	2	...
Gasoline, Unleaded	NYM	7.3	13.6	4	...
Swiss Franc	IMM	2.2	6.9	2	...
Coffee "C"	CSCE	11.0	10.2	1	...
Heating Oil #2	NYM	9.2	12.3	4	...
Cattle, Live	CME	2.8	10.1	8	..
Soybean Meal	CBT	4.6	8.4	5	..
Copper	CMX	13.6	23.6	3	.
Soybean Oil	CBT	4.5	8.8	9	.
Cotton #2	CTN	4.7	8.7	4	.
Wheat	CBT	4.1	11.1	8	.
British Pound (new) £	IMM	3.0	13.3	3	.
Pork Bellies	CME	7.3	4.3	3	.
Cocoa	CSCE	7.0	8.7	6	.
5-Year Treasury Notes	CBT	1.3	16.9	8	.
Canadian Dollar	IMM	0.8	4.8	4	.
Major Market Maxi Index	CBT	5.3	11.0	1	.
NYSE Composite Index	NYFE	4.7	12.1	2	.
US Treasury Bills	IMM	0.4	8.1	6	.
Municipal Bonds	CBT	1.4	7.5	4	.
Hogs	CME	4.4	10.4	10	.
Platinum	NYM	6.1	18.3	7	.
Wheat	KC	3.7	9.1	7	.
Cattle, Feeder	CME	2.3	7.0	5	.
U S Dollar Index	CNT	2.5	8.7	4	
Orange Juice	CTN	6.1	12.3	5	
Wheat	MPLS	3.6	9.0	7	
Value Line Average	KC	3.7	10.6	1	
Lumber	CME	3.0	12.8	10	
CRB Futures Price Index	NYFE	2.9	16.9	3	

Table 52.1 (Continued)

Commodity Futures	Exchange	% Margin	Effective % Margin	Contracts to Trade for Equal Dollar Profit	Relative Contract Liquidity
Silver	CBT	6.0	6.6	11	
Rapeseed (US $)	WPG	4.3	11.2	27	
Soybeans	MCE	3.8	9.4	19	

CBT	Chicago Board of Trade
CME	Chicago Mercantile Exchange
CMX	Commodity Exchange, New York
CSCE	Coffee. Sugar & Cocoa Exchange, New York
CTN	New York Cotton Exchange
IMM	International Monetary Market at CME, Chicago
KC	Kansas City Board of Trade
MCE	MidAmerica Commodity Exchange, Chicago
MPLS	Minneapolis Grain Exchange
	NYFE New York Futures Exchange (New York Stock Exchange)
NYM	New York Mercantile Exchange
WPG	Winnipeg Commodity Exchange

Margin source: REFCO, Inc.

This is a reference chart for speculators. It compares markets according to their per-contract potential for profit and how easily contracts can be bought or sold (i.e., trading liquidity). Each is a proportional measure and is meaningful only when compared to others in the same column.

The number in the "Contracts to Trade for Equal Dollar Profit" column shows how many contracts of one commodity must be traded to obtain the same potential return as another commodity. Contracts to Trade = (Tick $ value) × (3-year Maximum Price Excursion).

"Relative Contract Liquidity" places commodities in descending order according to how easily all of their contracts can be traded. Commodities at the top of the list are easiest to buy and sell, commodities at the bottom of the list are the most difficult. "Relative Contract Liquidity" is the number of contracts to trade times total open interest times a volume factor which is:

$$1 \text{ or } \exp\left(\frac{\ln(volume)}{\ln(5000)} - 2\right)$$

RULE 53

THE SMARTER YOU ARE, THE LONGER IT TAKES

Elsewhere in this book I discuss the old trader's rule of three tens. This rule said that a trader spends the first ten years of his life learning the business and scalping, the second ten years making money, and the third ten years managing that money in order to make more money.

It took much longer to become a success in the trading profession than I thought it would. I remember asking my supervisor at the First National Bank about taking a year's leave of absence so that I could trade futures for my own account. My request was denied, but I left the bank anyway and started my trading career in 1974. It took much longer than a year to make my fortune.

As in every profession or human endeavor, there are shortcuts to superficial success in trading. Some brokers churn their client equity to become high commission producers. Some traders pocket orders on the exchange floors, and some firm traders front run on orders. These are not the ones I consider to be successful in the real sense of the word. As an intelligent person you try to understand the basics of any situation: you ask who, what, when, where, and why. Once you understand a situation, you can apply it to another situation sometime in the future. This is what learning is about.

The markets, because they are composed of so many infinite variables, raise many more who, what, when, where, and why questions. This can create more confusion than clarification, yet it does not deny the need to know about the markets. In order to forecast imminent price moves, we absorb as much information as we can. There is a danger, however, if we go to the extreme and learn more than is needed to trade the markets successfully.

> *The key to wealth in trading is simplicity.*

I was up in the trading room of my clearing firm one Friday afternoon at the end of a tough week. I blurted out to a couple of traders nearby that I hadn't made any money that week because I was too smart for the game.

Can anyone be too smart for the trading game? The answer is yes. If you look at the markets in their simplest form, you realize that there are essentially only three actions you can perform: you buy it, you sell it, or you hold it. This is the beauty of the markets: There is no grey area where subjective judgment enters into the equation for correct analysis. Yet, the smarter ones among us are the first to look for the shadows.

If you buy something and it goes down, do you ask why or do you sell out? If you buy and it goes up, do you ask who is buying it or do you hang on? If you sell something short and it goes nowhere, do you wait for the next government report or do you close out your positions? The more intelligent you are, the more questions you have. We all think there is more to making money in the markets than buying, selling, and holding on.

I once taught a seminar on cyclic timing. A student in the seminar came up to me afterwards and told me that the had lost money trading on the Chicago Board Options Exchange. His mentor, who specialized in time spreads, told the student to watch the spreads that oscillated between a positive value and a negative value. He told the student to buy the spread when it oscillated in one direction and sell it out when it oscillated the other way. The student lost money.

As I listened to him, I immediately saw the problem: The spread oscillated back and forth. All he had to do was put on the spread at one price, wait, and leg out of the spread when it went the opposite way. He could be making several hundred thousand dollars a year doing this.

The key to wealth in trading is simplicity. My student was trained to believe that in order to make a lot of money he had to work very hard. In reality, the principles you use to make money on a one-lot trade are the same principles you would use to make money on a hundred-lot trade. You don't have to work harder to take on bigger positions, just more intelligently. And the more intelligently you work, the easier it becomes to make money.

There is an inherent irony to success in the trading business: When you really start to make money, it becomes boring because only certain trading strategies and styles work in the market. Once you find a way to make money consistently, you cannot attempt to optimize your strategy. The more you optimize a trading strategy, the more market-specific it becomes. When the markets change, you will be stranded with a fully optimized strategy that is now looking for a market condition under which it can be traded successfully. When successful trading becomes boring, it becomes difficult to continue making money.

I've grouped together a few trading ideas to keep in mind, even after you have learned all you can about the markets.

1. If you have a game plan, stick with it.
2. If you want to trade in a bull market, always buy.
   Don't ever sell a bull market to get a position in it. Wait until the market reacts to get to a lower buying level.
3. If your mind is wandering all the time, watch a few more markets to keep busy. Bored minds open up closed wallets.
4. Develop outside activities. Read books, exercise often, and do things that can take your mind off of trading.
5. Isolate yourself from others who trade with their opinions because you don't want their opinions to become your own.
6. Don't tamper with your positions once they show profits.
7. Keep the winners and figure out ways to get rid of the losers.

If worse comes to worse and your mind is wandering all over the place getting you into losing trading situations, think about this: When you get older and your mind finally starts to slow down, you'll become a successful trader.

RULE 54

IT IS HARDER TO GET OUT OF A TRADE THAN TO GET INTO ONE

Over the years of instructions to novice traders I have always heard the complaint that they can get into a trade correctly, but they can never get out of a trade correctly. When these novice traders become traders with average skills, the complaints lessen but still persist.

When average traders become superior traders, they complain about bad fills or about missing the sell or buy signals, but they never complain about not being able to get out of the markets correctly.

After thorough analysis, I determined why novice traders complain about not being able to get out of a trade correctly, regardless of it being a winner or loser, but seldom complain about getting into a trade correctly. The reason is that there are more opportunities to get into a trade than to get out of one, regardless of whether the trade was successful or not.

The tools needed to make a decision to enter into a trade are completely different from those needed to exit trades. Deciding whether or not to enter a trade involves making a probability analysis. A skilled trader analyzes a situation for its profit and loss potential before deciding whether or not to enter a trade. Because the trader is using these entry tools on a trade that doesn't yet exist, the trader uses his or her total knowledge of the market to analyze many different situations for opportunities. In the course of a trading week, there may be about 15 or 20 such opportunities passing by an intermediate-term trader.

Once the trader enters a trade, he or she no longer has 15 or 20 profit opportunities to consider. The trader now has only one position to manage. However, some traders mistakenly apply the many technical techniques to an analyzing exit points of a single trade that they put on. *They are trying to maintain an opportunistic approach to the management of the trade.*

> **The tools needed to make a decision to enter into a trade are completely different from those needed to exit trades.**

A good trader understands this distinction—the analysis of opportunities before the trade versus the management of the one trade after the trade is entered into. A superior trader knows how to manage that one trade for maximum profit.

There is only one way to manage a trade: If it shows a profit, let it run; if it shows a loss, find an exit point to limit the losses. The successful trader uses many techniques to enter a trade but uses only loss limitation techniques to exit a losing trade. The unsuccessful trader uses many techniques to enter a trade and uses many of the same techniques to remove him- or herself from winning trades! For instance, a trader might sell out at a small profit, having sold the high, only to find out later that the market continued to move in the direction of the previous trade. The trader could have made a larger profit had he not used entry techniques to exit the trade.

RULE 55

DON'T TALK ABOUT WHAT YOU'RE DOING IN THE MARKETS

If you want to discuss your trades, do so only after they are closed out and you have taken your profits or losses, but never before. I learned this lesson in 1974 from a trader named Harold Goodman at the Chicago Open Board of Trade.

In 1974, the young turks in the mini pits were traders who eventually went over to the major exchanges and established fame and further fortune: Richard Dennis, Tommy Willis, Jack Savage, and David Ware. Richard Dennis eventually became one of the biggest traders at the Chicago Board of Trade. He recently retired from managing money after making more than $200 million for his own trading account. Tommy Willis eventually found a partner and managed money. He still trades actively. David Ware made more than a million dollars in a year in which a million dollars was still considered money. He invested his money in California real estate in the 1970s.

These traders had one thing in common when it came to trading: They all relied on Harold Goodman for advice and expertise. Harold wrote a weekly newsletter for a company that was then known as Greene & Collins. Collins later took his operation to the Chicago Board of Trade and is now associated with Les Roenthal in the firm of Rosenthal-Collins. Harold wrote one of the best newsletters in the industry. He had one of the sharpest trading minds that I ever encountered. While the young turks were learning the business, Harold was going about doing his: trading the primary trends. The Open Board of Trade traded job-lot-sized contracts of the primary markets, grains, meats, currencies, and options. The size of the contracts traded has no bearing on the trends of the markets. As long as Harold could buy all he wanted in bull markets and sell all he wanted in bear markets, he was happy and extremely profitable.

One day I was in the wheat minipit at the market close and the traders were evening up their positions. Harold walked into the pit, and Willis, Dennis, and Ware immediately began offering wheat and soybeans to him. Harold pulled out a bunch of trading cards and started carding down the offers. I later found out that he took everything the young turks sold. The next morning wheat opened lower. Soybeans opened unchanged to slightly higher. Corn opened steady and traded lower. Harold was at his trading desk on the floor watching the grains open. As the day progressed, the wheat stopped selling off, then firmed up, and then moved above the settlement price. Towards the end of the day, wheat, soybeans, and corn closed limit up. Ten minutes before the minimarkets closed, Harold walked into the pits and made offers to buy more corn and soybeans. He was one of those traders who knew the main trend of the markets he was trading and added to those positions. He had a conviction in the direction of the markets and he followed it religiously.

He knew what he was doing, and because he was the biggest trader at the Open Board, he served as an out for the smaller traders. If Willis and Dennis couldn't unload their inventory or cover their shorts before the markets closed, they would find Harold willing to take the other side. He would bail them out of bad position.

An episode involving one of Harold's orders illustrated how he dealt with the people on the trading floor. Harold was long silver contracts, and silver prices were making new highs daily. He took a vacation in Hawaii and called his clearing firm from there to inquire about this positions. The telephone connection was very bad; a second and third connection showed no improvement. Before hanging up, Harold told the clerk to buy 1,000 silver contracts. Afterwards, it occurred to the clerk that he didn't know whether Harold meant to buy 1,000 contracts of Open Board silver, which traded in 1,000 ounces per contract, or 1,000 Chicago Board of Trade silver, which traded in 5,000 ounces per contract. The order was either for 1 million ounces of silver or for 5 million ounces. The clerk attempted to reach Harold in Hawaii, but he was nowhere to be found. To be safer than sorrier, the clerk executed the order for 1 million ounces of silver. Silver went up and the clerk wondered whether the order had been for 5 million.

> *I learned from many hard knocks to keep my mouth shut about my positions.*

Harold came back from Hawaii and checked his purchase and sale statements. He had wanted to buy 5 million ounces of silver. The clerk was in trouble—very expensive trouble. Silver prices had climbed 40¢ an ounce since the 1 million ounces were purchased. The clerk could find himself having to come up with the 4 million ounces of appreciated silver, totaling $1.6 million.

When the clerk told Harold the mistake, do you know what Harold did? He patted the clerk on the back and told him not to make such a mistake again, bad connection or no bad connection. He turned around and gave the same clerk an order to buy the 4 million ounces of silver that he didn't buy 40¢ lower. Harold was that type of trader. He knew the weaknesses and strengths of people and worked around them. He was a loner who had learned to rely only on himself. As such, he was harsher on himself than on others.

I learned many trading lessons from Harold, but one of the most memorable is from years ago. I am extremely fond of repeating one particular lesson to young traders—never talking about trades while I have them on.

Soybeans were strong one day, so I bought a few contracts. The prices whipped around the whole day and made me extremely nervous. After the close, I went over to the broadtape and looked for stories dealing with soybeans. The cash prices from the Midwest showed improvement. Export demand was good. Supplies were being drawn down. An extremely bullish scenario Yet rumors swirled through the pit about a higher than expected production report due out the next day. The rumors had me on edge.

I walked over to Harold's desk on the trading floor. He was writing his weekly marketletter. I had spoken a few words to Harold in the months that I was at the exchange, but he didn't really know me. He looked up and asked me what I wanted.

I screwed up enough courage to ask him what was really on my mind. I wanted to find out what his position in soybeans was, whether he was long or short. If he was long, I would agree with him. If he were short, I would try to persuade him to think bullishly. I didn't ask him what his total position was. I asked him if he was long. The way I phrased my question I hoped he would take the cue that I was also long. If he said that he was long millions of bean contracts and that he wanted to buy more tomorrow morning, I would feel reassured. Instead, he threw down his pen, looked me in the eyes, and yelled out, "It's none of your god damn business!" He folded his hands behind his head, leaned back on his chair and yelled again, "What business is it of yours to know what my position is?"

He must have felt my shock and embarrassment, for he softened his tone a little and said, "I have a position in beans and it's a big position. If you know my position, what can you do to help it? And if you don't know my position, what can you do to hurt it?

"If I tell you my position, which might be the opposite of your position, are you going to argue with me that you are right and I am wrong? Imagine if you can convince me that I am wrong. Are you going to be here tomorrow to tell me what to do with my position?

"If your position is the same as mine, are you going to give me some of your profits, or am I supposed to give you some of mine? Your knowing my position won't do a damn bit of good for it. In fact, your knowing will even distract me from maintaining an even keel in this play. Okay, Bill?"

At the time, the shock of being corrected by Harold prevented me from absorbing the impact of his words. Over the years I thought about what he said and it started to make sense. I learned from many hard knocks to keep my mouth shut about my positions. I had a tendency to be swayed by others' comments and opinions. If someone could come up with a better argument and analysis than I had, I was more than willing to reverse my positions on the next morning's opening bell. I learned that if I did that, I wouldn't have a game plan and I wouldn't know what to do afterwards. If I stuck with my own analysis, in the worst possible scenario I would at least have a feel of what to do. If I followed others' analyses, I had to rely on them.

Friends no longer ask me about my positions. When others offer to tell me about their positions, I nod and walk away. If they persist, I change the subject. I don't want to tell others about my positions and I don't want to know about theirs.

RULE 56

WE ALL MAKE MISTAKES, BUT WE MUSTN'T ALLOW OUR EMOTIONS TO OBSTRUCT OUR LEARNING PROCESS

You confront many situations in the trading arena in which you most likely make the wrong choices and lose money. In retrospect, there is only one straight and narrow path for making money in the markets. On that path you'll be traversing a lot of other paths which will cause you to make mistakes. Most of these sidepaths are not financial disasters, but any one of them can be if you allow them.

For example, a sidepath which might distract you from trading successfully could be as simple as your being fixated on some specific trading strategy. I know some people who have hooked onto using Japanese Candlestick charting and have made it their mission to study every aspect of it. Candlestick charting is a set of specific daily price patterns which forecast future price movements. Others have fixated on using moving averages and have become experts at every nuance of these momentum indicators. Once these techniques start to overwhelm you to the exclusion of anything else, then you've allowed these to become more important than the real reason to trade or invest in the markets: to make money.

Similar to Hindu philosophy, in the trading world you will continue to make the same mistakes over and over again until

Don't personalize market rejection by rejecting yourself as a person.

you get it right. Then you must remove the mistakes from obstructing your success. You can become successful only by undergoing this initial trial and error period and then making a conscious effort to remove your obstructions.

Each of us has a particular background. We've grown up in different environments. In the process of using the support systems our parents have given to us, we are able to achieve our objectives. I'm not discussing the fact that some of us may not know what our objectives are. The floundering that most of us have experienced in our youth merely represents attempts at finding goals and objectives worth achieving. These attempts aren't necessarily failures but a way to eliminate less necessary goals and objectives.

Depending on our emotional and psychological makeup, what we consider to be less than desirable as a goal might be highly treasured by others. This isn't even an issue of right or wrong. It's an issue of discovering what is out there that can provide enough motivation for you to seek it out and perfect it.

A danger rests in the following scenario, however. In the process of eliminating less than desirable goals we go through the process of working with those goals, striving for them, and when the objectives are within reach, achieving them doesn't always satisfy us as we expected. Was pursuing them a mistake? Of course not. They're part of our own search for our own truths, our own personal objectives.

In trading the markets there are many actions you can create to make yourself more successful, i.e., make money in the markets. There are many different ways to tackle that objective. Some of us initially, because of our inexperience in the trading business, get sidetracked on the way to achieving the ultimate goal by the excitement and thrills of the chase. The game itself becomes the goal.

Choosing the game itself as the goal is neither right nor wrong if that's what you're really after. Many times I've confronted unsuccessful traders, those who weren't able to make money. I asked them what they would like to do rather than battle it out every day in the pits or from the upstairs trading

241

room. Few are honest enough, or even conscious enough of their actions, to say that they would rather be doing something else. The few who do recognize and can verbalize it eventually wind up doing something else. This is their continued search to satisfy their needs.

Like any profession, successful trading isn't always thrilling. It entails a large degree of boredom. The exhilaration and excitement of risk-prone trading that we are led to believe to be "correct" trading is only the peripheral elements of trading. Yes, you can let these two elements of trading be the driving force to your trading. Unless you address the point that trading is often humdrum, then you will never be able to make money in the markets.

Mistakes, therefore, are the results of unsatisfactory searches for satisfying your goals and objectives. That's all they are.

It's only when you attach feelings of rejection to mistakes that there are problems in your search for goals. You mustn't do this.

If you attach personal rejection to your mistake, you condition yourself to eliminate undesirable goals less efficiently. Why is this so? When you personalize market rejection into a rejection of you as a person, you will build up defense mechanisms which will shield you from personal sensitivities. This will prevent you from looking at problems objectively in the future. Frankly, it hurts to be rejected personally. In the process of building up the defense mechanisms, you create extended responses. So instead of taking loss in your position because it went against you, you're saying to yourself that the position should be held because the market reports were wrong. Once you deceive yourself by believing the market reports weren't aligned to your position, it's not that difficult for you to think that other factors beyond your obvious control influenced those developments. When does it stop? When should it stop? Certainly not further away from the source of your problem: your losing position. The best way to deal with your losing position is to get rid of it as soon as possible. The chain from action to reaction becomes more complex and distracting. Eventually it will even lengthen more. You will have allowed the problem and the solution to the problem to be separated from each other. As a result, future attempts at resolving the germinated problem really become difficult!

RULE 57

CONTROL WHAT YOU CAN, MANAGE WHAT YOU CANNOT

Traders who are unsuccessful in the markets do not understand their roles in relation to the market's perspective. Traders are small players in the context of the market's overall existence. Not only must they recognize this fact, they also must never think otherwise. No matter how much money the trader has to invest in the market, the market is the market.

Which aspects of investing and speculating does the trader control, and what does he have no say in? When does a trader switch from a leader to a follower? How important is it to a trader's success to know when and how to follow or lead?

The following are items that the trader can, and must, control:

- The amount of money put into the markets.
- The number of markets to follow.
- When to enter a trade.
- How to enter a trade.
- When to exit a trade.
- How to exit a trade.
- How to spend one's time.

There is no need to determine probabilities that a trader has a certain amount of capital to put into the market or when he enters into a trade. There is 100% certainty that the trader can put X amount into the markets and can put in a trade on, say, Monday morning 5 minutes and 30 seconds after the first trade in soybeans.

The following are items over which the trader has absolutely no control:

- The direction markets will move.
- The duration of the markets' movements.

> *The market moves whenever and however it wants to. If the trader believes he can dictate to the market when and how he wants it to move, surprises occur.*

Failure to recognize these aspects of the markets early will result in failure at trading. And the irony is that a trader will end his career without knowing why he failed.

Problems occur, and failures materialize, when the trader starts to believe that the power which comes with controlling what he can control can be exercised in situations over which he has no control. The market moves whenever and however it wants to. If the trader believes he can dictate to the market when and how he wants it to move, surprises occur.

The mere act of buying or selling a futures contract or a stock implies that you want that particular instrument to move up or down. When you buy, you want it to go up. When you sell, you want it to go down. What is mistaken is the fact that when you buy and it goes up, you are really buying something that is already strong. Your buying does not make it stronger.

One act of buying or selling has no extended impact on the market. Except for the extreme case where individual buying or selling can actually move the market when others follow in concerted action, it is impossible to buy and have the market go up immediately afterward, or sell and have the market go down immediately.

You were there at the right time and right place. In the worst scenario of timing, you merely followed the market, and in the best scenario, you anticipated the market's move. In either case, you had no control over it. If you weren't the one who bought the lows or sold the highs, it would have been some other person. And if the market didn't move after you bought or sold, it would have eventually, independent of your actions.

A friend related an incident many years ago which illustrates the subject of this chapter explicitly. Ralph Peters was Chairman of the Chicago Board of Trade around the time I became a member of the exchange. (He passed away recently at the age of 56. His estate was valued at between $300 and $500 million. Once these numbers are reached, who cares if you give or take a couple hundred million?)

A broker friend had been following the recently initiated trading in S&P 500 futures at the Chicago Mercantile Exchange. My friend's eclectic and highly mathematical calculations determined that a critical number would be a strong resistance point. He got his clients short just below the critical point and placed stop buy orders several ticks above the critical point to protect this clients' short positions.

The market was bullish, continually making higher highs and higher lows. This one particular day's trading activity showed strength. It reached up just shy of the critical number and sold off. It reached up again to a fraction higher than before and then sold off. The second sell-off stopped short of the first reaction's low. A higher low pattern formed. For the third rally it stalled right at the critical number. There was obvious interest at that critical number because prices churned around at that number for minutes, which seemed like hours.

Boom. The critical number did not hold. In rapid succession trades went across a tick above the critical number, then another quote a tick higher.

Only after the market made new highs by four ticks did it exhaust itself and back off. As the selling came back into the market, prices dropped below the critical number. My friend, astonished at the market's drive to reach his stops, cursed his bad luck.

My friend waited for the fills on his stop buy orders. He waited. Still no fills. He wondered whether or not the clerks misplaced his orders and perhaps he luckily has not been stopped out of his initial shorts. He called down to the floor a half hour after the market closed and requested fills.

The clerk reported that the fills on the stops were canceled and described the scene on the floor several hours earlier when the market pushed past the critical number. Ralph Peters had also been watching that critical number from his office. However, he watched it from the perspective of a person wanting to challenge it, not of a person following the markets. The first time the market moved close to the critical number, he had discretely entered buy orders. The second time it got up fractionally higher he had also been a discrete buyer. But the third time he tested his will against the market's omnipotence. He entered an order to buy 1,000 contracts right at the critical number, the first time in S&P futures contract trading history that such an order was entered.

The locals panicked and bought everything they could. They pushed the market higher and caught all the stops several ticks above the critical number.

After the 1,000 contract had been filled, along with a bunch of others around that price level, other brokers at the other side of the trading pit screamed that they had thousands of sell orders—below the critical number. There was no way that any orders could trade above these resting orders, given the supply of contracts offered for sale.

The pit canceled the highest tick, then the next highest, all the way down to the critical number. Prices on market orders were lowered to adjust the fills to reflect the new lower day's high. Limit stop buy orders above the adjusted high were now canceled. My friend's orders to stop buy were never filled.

The market had a critical number to resist any further up move for the time being. One person tried to bull the market into submission and failed. This incident illustrates the fact that there are things that a trader can control and things that he cannot. There are things that are strictly in the province of the market and can never be broached even by one of the best speculators.

The day's high eventually gave way to further up-moves, but only when the market was ready to let it do so. And not before. In the case of this trader, the losses he sustained were controlled. For the price of several hundred thousand dollars, he found out what he could not control. He could not control the market. This lesson was cheap compared to the money that he was eventually able to accumulate.

As far as your own trading is concerned, make sure that if and when you get a ridiculous scheme to move the markets that the money you have at stake is what you can afford to lose. If not, save yourself the aggravation and look for another career.

CONCLUSION

THE 360-DEGREE WHEEL THEORY

Market knowledge is an accumulation of many experiences. The rules that I have gathered in this book have been developed by expert market minds. I have merely applied them to current markets.

The 57 rules that I have elaborated on in this book became known to me in 1971, the first year I traded the markets. Over the last 18 years I have journeyed into stocks, options, and futures markets and learned as much about the ramifications of these rules as I could without an instructor at my side. Around the ninth year of my journey into market knowledge some of the rules that I learned in the first year started to make sense.

A case in point is the old saying that the only way to make a small fortune in the commodity markets is to start with a large fortune. When I heard this saying in the first year of my career, my first reaction was to laugh at the cynicism inherent in the statement. I thought the rule stated that if I wanted to make $500,000 in the markets, I had to start with $1 million. By the time I finished trading and lost half of my startup capital, I would have wound up with the other half, that is, the small fortune.

Years of trading experience have taught me to reinterpret that statement not as cynicism, but as common sense money management. Embedded in the statement is the key to market survival: In order to make a better than average return, you need a large enough sum to trade and manage. To make $500,000 all you need is a 50 percent annualized return on a

248

larger fortune, the $1 million. The original statement means to say that you cannot make $500,000 yearly by starting with $25,000. The original sum has to be larger.

If I only knew then what I know now . . .

Another rule that I eventually interpreted correctly is Rule 38 in this book: Always buy new highs. I wrote that I always lost money when I did this. I had to sell out the longs I bought at new high prices after the markets retraced. I eventually found out that the action of buying the high was part

> *To make a better than average return, you need a large enough sum to trade and manage.*

of a more complete trading strategy. You have to be long at lower prices before you can buy new highs with safety. Buying new highs in itself is foolish and can only guarantee that prices will retrace and hand you losses. However, if buying new highs is adding to long positions accumulated at lower prices, then you cannot help but make money from the total position in bullish markets. This rule made trading sense when I saw it from a larger perspective.

Perspective is what makes traders successful. The ability to see these single sentence rules in the larger perspective of a trading paradigm helps traders succeed in markets.

The 360-degree wheel theory breaks down a trader's career into three time periods. In the first ten years you learn the rules and see how they play out in the markets. You don't know their exact meaning, but you do know what they sometimes work. At other times they fail miserably, like the rule of buying new highs. During this stage your thought is to buy new highs.

As the second decade starts, you see the same rules from a slightly different perspective, one with more depth. Your rule to buy new highs now reads like this: Buy new highs, but use your experience to isolate market events with discrimination. Before reaching this stage of the learning curve, you applied the rule indiscriminately.

Finally, on the third trip around the wheel, you are wiser still in your knowledge of the markets. The rules have remained the same, but the number of exceptions is greater. Now you can discard the application of certain rules under certain market conditions, whereas before, you applied the rules all the time, with a careful eye to the exceptions. At this point you are truly a wise speculator.

If you are fortunate and persistent enough to make it past the first revolution of knowledge, you will make money in the markets. If you are good enough to make it past the second revolution of experience, you can impart your knowledge to others. And if you are wise enough to make it past the third revolution of wisdom, you will indeed retire a very wealthy person.

INDEX